AF471721

Weeping Willow

Lessons of Loss and Love

Michelle Scavarda

authorHOUSE®

AuthorHouse™
1663 Liberty Drive
Bloomington, IN 47403
www.authorhouse.com
Phone: 1-800-839-8640

First published by AuthorHouse 7/15/2011

ISBN: 978-1-4634-3896-8 (e)
ISBN: 978-1-4634-3897-5 (dj)
ISBN: 978-1-4634-3898-2 (sc)

Library of Congress Control Number: 2011912117

Printed in the United States of America

To my siblings; it is because of you that I even have these stories to share. It is to all of you, Christopher, Annamarie and Matthew that I dedicate this special book!

Prologue

We all jumped in, excited about the ride, and I soon found myself stuck—stuck in a two-seater roller coaster car with my two siblings in front of me, my parents behind me and nobody next to me. I wanted out desperately but knew that wasn't a possibility as soon as the train slowly crept away from the station. It was gut-wrenching, heartbreaking and, quite honestly, the longest roller coaster ride I had ever been on. It was the first roller coaster I had to ride on by myself since my brother had died, and I wished for it to be the last. Deep down inside of me, I felt him there, next to me, with his hands up and a bright smile on his face. Somehow, that made it a little more painful, to feel he was there with me, though I couldn't see him, and I couldn't hear him.

Have you ever just sat down and thought about how the time has either gone by so incredibly slow or impossibly fast? It always seems to be that the best times of your life go by in the blink of an eye, and those times in your life which you wish would go by just as quickly seem to creep by as slowly as you think time could possibly go. For the past ten years, I have spent my life on one big roller coaster called *Time*. There have been several large inclines and straight down drops that lead into loops or corkscrews, as well as some little hills that popped me out of my seat and quickly brought me back down.

Roller coasters and theme parks are some of my family's favorite things to do, and mine! Find the craziest coaster and the most intense thrill ride and I will be there as soon as I can. There's just something about the rush

I get just before a ride begins that I absolutely love, or maybe it's simply built in me since I have been going on thrill rides since I was two years old. You're probably thinking, *Thrill rides at two years old?* But obviously they were the kiddy thrill rides you would find at most amusement parks.

My dad grew up going to theme parks and loving roller coasters himself so when I was born, being my parents' first child, he was all too excited about getting me onto my first wooden kiddy coaster at Rye Playland in Rye, New York. I have been addicted ever since. My siblings grew up the same way and enjoy our family trips that involve some sort of thrill ride, especially my favorite place on earth, Disney World. Those trips are the memories my siblings and I will be sharing with our own children someday. As much as I love roller coasters, I can honestly say that this life roller coaster, *Time,* is one that tossed me around a little too much for my liking. Losing a sibling has had it's up and down days and has been quite the journey.

This book was written in hope that it may touch even just one other person's life, and to open the world to the experience of sibling loss, giving those who have lost a sibling a voice. I have always felt that compared to all the losses one could experience, there hasn't been as much written about the loss of a sibling, let alone an in-depth account. I wanted the world to see the inside story of my own grief and loss, hoping that reading my story will somehow reach another's life and they will feel less alone in their process.

Admittedly, writing this book has also allowed me to continue healing in my own way. I have done numerous things, as you will find out further in the book, to help me heal, but I have found that writing has been one of the most therapeutic tools I have. Writing has brought new experiences and feelings, enlightening me about my very own core.

Whether you've lost a sibling or someone else you dearly love, you are now in good company. It can be difficult to bring yourself back to your most painful moments in life, but remember that as you immerse yourself in each chapter and turn each page, we are in this together. We're in this as you begin reading these words, as the words become more applicable to your own life, and finally we're in this together until this small fragment of life while reading this book is closed, and a new chapter, a new book is opened.

I hope that in reading *Weeping Willow* you will find comfort, peace of mind, be inspired and learn something new about yourself. I know I did. Peace be with you on your continued life journey.

Author
Michelle Scavarda

Siblinghood

"Our brothers and sisters are there with us
from the dawn of our personal stories to the inevitable dusk."
~ Susan Scarf Merrell ~

I come from a fairly large family and I'd have it no other way. There's just something warm about knowing someone is always there when you're part of a big family. I am the oldest of four children. Including me, there are two girls and two boys. In order, it's myself, Christopher, Annamarie and Matthew. Chris is two years younger than I am, Anna is five years younger, and Matt is nine years younger than I am. My mom has four siblings, and my dad has two, so including both sides of my family, all together, I have sixteen first cousins. I love each of my family members so very much and am so proud to be a part of this family. You know those funny little stories that weren't meant to be funny but are hysterical and only your family busts a gut laughing at them? I could spend hours with you telling stories like that about my siblings or my cousins…but I won't right at this moment!

Because my brother Chris and I are only two years apart, we spent the most time together, and not always the most wanted time. We were in the same schools at the same time, hung out with many of the same friends, and helped watch over our two youngest siblings when needed. Chris was by far the biggest daredevil in our family, always coming up with some new idea on how to make life more exciting. One winter, after the movie *Home Alone* came out, he thought he'd try what the character, Kevin, did by sledding down the hallway stairs and out the front door. Our stairs are set up much like the McAlister family's in the movie, being that they are directly in line with the front door. He took his blue, plastic sled up the staircase and told me to hold the front door open; he was coming down. And there he went with his mouth wide open screaming his head off, down the stairs, out the front door, flying over the porch steps and stopping inches from the fairly busy road we live on. Needless to say, our mom nearly had a heart attack when she saw him fly out the front door.

My sister, Anna, has always been known as the quiet, sweet young girl out in public, but at home she has the voice of a lion. I shared a room with her until my junior and senior years of high school and for those of you girls who have a sister, you know all too well what it is like "sharing" clothes, and taking up each other's space. Although you cannot miss her around the house, she is always quick to ask if you're okay if ever there is something wrong. Anna was quite gullible growing up and believed pretty much whatever Chris and I told her as well as anything she heard. One time Anna came in from playing in the backyard one afternoon to tell Dad that she heard God speaking to her. She was rather excited and Dad asked her what was said. "Hello Anna, this is God talking," she said. Dad looked at her, perplexed, and asked where she heard God talk to her. She pointed towards a large maple tree on the right hand side of our yard, "Over there!" she exclaimed. As Dad looked over, he saw Chris nearly at the top of the tree, giggling that he'd gotten his little sister to believe he was God talking to her.

The age difference between my sister and me as kids seemed huge, and the same goes for my brother, Matt. He always seemed so little to me. No matter how much older he got, he would still be the littlest brother. He was always doing something cute or funny and with no intention of making it that way. We had gone out to dinner one night with family friends when Matt was around five years old. While sitting at the table, someone told a joke that children wouldn't understand. Matt kept asking what everyone was talking about and Dad said to him, "Oh, it's okay, Matthew, I don't think you'd understand, it's over your head." Matt was rather offended by his comment and began defending himself. "You know, Dad," he began, "I'm sitting down. If I stand up, it won't be over my head anymore." Matt always made us laugh, that's for sure, and he followed his three older siblings around all the time but mostly his big brother, Chris.

For the most part, we all got along fairly well despite the fights and brawls our parents saw. My goodness, did we have some big ones, and who mainly got the blame for most incidences? Usually it was Chris or

I, whichever one hadn't really done it. Nevertheless, isn't that the way it usually goes with siblings? As a child, you smirk when you think you've gotten away with something that you did wrong but then it's completely unfair to you when you get the blame for something one of your brothers or sisters did. Oh, the joys of having siblings. But really, there are so many wonderful times and they outweigh all the teasing, punching, and shouting. I would do anything in my capability for my siblings, as well as I know they would do the same for me.

Road Trip!

"And that's the wonderful thing about family travel: it provides you with experiences that will remain locked forever in the scar tissue of your mind."
~ Dave Barry ~

My grandparents on my mom's side live in Florida, about forty-five minutes away from Disney World, and my family visits them from our home in Westchester, New York, at least once every year. This place, by far, is my favorite place to go, as it is my siblings'. I always felt like I was in a fairy tale when I was there, not only at Disney but the property my grandparents live on. It is an escape from reality and the truth that the world holds.

You may think we are crazy but the six of us drive down in our van for just about an eighteen-hour trip. Nothing is better than spending a full day fidgeting and whining in the car with your family...Not! The drives were rough when we were really little, but as we got older, spending the time together in close vicinity wasn't really that bad. In fact, it was pretty fun!

Dad used to set up the back seats with sleeping bags and pillows so that he could keep driving at night while we slept. We thought this was the coolest thing because when we woke up we were usually almost there. On one occasion when Matt was still in diapers, we woke up and he stunk so badly and was in dire need of a change. We were about five minutes from grandma's house. Chris and I were rolling him back and forth over the backseat bench because none of us (including Anna in the backbench with Chris) wanted to be next to a stinky diaper boy.

We could not stop laughing and we knew we were almost to our favorite place. We were all suddenly best friends when we arrived down there no matter what time it was; it was one of the best feelings in the entire world. Even if we quarreled down there, it didn't seem as important or huge as when we were at home. Our surroundings just pulled us in.

The land my grandparents live on was passed down in the family and they moved down there after living in Northport on Long Island, New York. Because of it being passed down, the land is very different from most pieces of property you would find available in Florida. This two-acre piece of land is surrounded by beautiful palm trees and various other tropical trees to the point where you can just barely see neighboring land and the busy road they live near. You cannot see their house from the road which makes it that much more peaceful. It is quite cool because of the shade the trees give and very serene.

My grandparents designed the house and built it after they retired. It is a one-floor house with three bedrooms and a beautiful back porch looking out into their densely wooded backyard. Minutes away from their home is a quiet freshwater spring in the depths of Florida's forests, very refreshing to say the least. The water is constantly being naturally pumped from underground and the temperature stays at 72°F year round. It is definitely a place to get away to; and what's better than being forty-five minutes away from Disney World, being able to go when we wanted? What a dream come true for any kid, and how happy we always were in this place.

Riding Into A Nightmare

"What we remember from childhood we remember forever - permanent ghosts, stamped, inked, imprinted, eternally seen."
~ Cynthia Ozick ~

I am currently twenty-six years old in 2011 and have been to Florida more times than my age; so many times that I cannot remember what happened on what trip and what year each one was. We have driven down with different aunts and uncles and for various holidays. On several trips we have met other family members living down in Florida for some great fun whether at Disney or at the beach.

One year we even met our close family friends, who are also our neighbors, right in the heart of Disney's Magic Kingdom for a full day of absolute fun together. Every year we would come back from Florida sharing with them, Frank (my age) and Maryann, a year older than Anna, and their parents how great it is. It was exciting to finally get to spend time together down there and create the memories that we did.

When we all went to dinner, taking a break from the rides, dessert was what all the kids looked forward to. We all got dirt and worms (crushed cookies and gummies) with our dinner meals. When it arrived, Chris and Frank convinced Matt that he was really going to eat dirt and worms. He was rather upset and insisted on getting another dessert. Frank and Chris thought they were clever because they were going to eat the extra dessert themselves but were disappointed when the dessert was given to Frank's sister, Maryann. I couldn't finish mine and Anna couldn't finish hers, so we both gave ours to Maryann too, who accepted the desserts with excitement. She had her own dessert plus three others and loved every bit of them.

We finished eating and immediately went straight for the hour and a half wait for Splash Mountain. There, we waited in line as Chris and Frank began to strike up a conversation with a girl from Georgia. They thought they were being slick until the little sister, Maryann, who just had four deserts, pushes her way through our group, up to Chris and Frank. She was extremely hyper and began telling her life story at warp speed to the Georgia girl. "Hi, my name is Maryann and I live at…in New York. This is my older brother and these are our neighbors, Chris and Michelle. We're here in Disney…" Her story went on. The boys were mortified that she would scare the cute girl away. If the Georgia girl didn't think we, as New Yorkers, talked fast before, she did now. Each trip has its own unforgettable story that will be told for years.

Florida trips, the stories and memories are all precious and priceless to me. My family has been so fortunate enough to have a wonderful place to stay in Florida without having to pay the normal expenses of a vacation. There have been some years that I remember being down there to celebrate my birthday at the beginning of March. How amazing it was to be down there at the very end of February when it was so cold and snowy in New York. Although as a kid I loved the snow, it was nice to have a warm, sunny break.

One Florida trip that I will always have imbedded in my memory was February of 2000. We went down with such great expectations for a relaxing vacation and drove right into a fairy tale dream. What we didn't know was that this was not a fairy tale which would have a "happily ever after." We had no idea we would be riding back into a nightmare.

The Happiest Place On Earth

"If you can dream it, you can do it."
~ Walt Disney ~

The last week of February 2000, my family and I took our yearly trip down to Florida. I was 14, Chris 12, Anna 9, and Matt was 5. We arrived, unloaded and, of course, went straight to the freshwater springs to soak up the Florida atmosphere. Who could simply resist? The second we were done, my siblings and I asked my dad when we we were going to Disney because Florida would not be the same without it! We planned out the day(s) we wanted to go, the park(s) we want to go to and then planned around that fantastic day. This particular year we went to Epcot, the Magic Kingdom, and Sea World.

When it came to thrill rides and exhilarating activities, Chris was a daredevil, even more so than I was. I love intense rides but sometimes it would take some talking into by him for me to go on one. Together, we were always trying to get Anna on rides that she was just tall enough for; sometimes she wouldn't budge and other times we could coerce her into joining us.

On one trip, we tried so incredibly hard to get her on *The Tower of Terror* but she was refusing without some sort of bribe. In thinking that she would forget how we got her on the ride, Chris offered to buy her a T-shirt with a picture of the ride on it, and I told her that she could play with my "untouchable" porcelain dolls when we got back home in New York. That sealed the deal for her but, of course, our parents didn't know about the bribes until after we got her on the ride. They laughed at us when we all got off and Anna said, "Where's my T-shirt"? Needless to say, our parents made sure Chris and I went through with our end of the bargain.

Chris and I were always striving for both of our younger siblings to get on every ride they possibly could. This particular year, in 2000, Matt was transitioning between the kiddy rides and the awesome, higher thrill ones. You have to be 48 inches tall to be able to get on most of the larger rides. We weren't sure if Matt would make it so we stuffed his little shoes with soft toilet paper because we thought it would give him a few more inches. Sure enough, he was just tall enough to ride all the Big Mountains: Space Mountain, Thunder Mountain and Splash Mountain. My dad was so ecstatic that Matt could get on all the rides that he took him by his little hand and practically dragged him up to the end of the queue in excitement. Chris and I giggled, knowing very well why our brother was able to get on the rides. At the end of the night, my dad carried Matt into bed and found the crumpled up toilet paper when he took off his shoes. "Oh, so that's why he was able to get on all those rides!" he said with a chuckle and then proceeded to stare Chris and me down with a smile and a look that said, *I know you two were behind this.*

The day we went to Sea World was on the chillier side for Floridians and other Southerners. It was a gorgeous day for us and we enjoyed the park not being so packed because of the "cold" weather. There weren't a lot of people there that day and the lines were short. We walked right on most rides and only waited five to ten minutes for others. In 2000, they had a new ride, *Journey to Atlantis*, a water ride. There were so many little surprises and we just loved it. We went on all together once and then Chris and I went on it repeatedly. I cannot count the amount of times we got off and then right back on!

The last day we were in Florida, on the 25th of February, we all celebrated my fifteenth birthday, which was six days later because of leap year. Grandma would always make me whatever dinner and cake I wanted; she spoiled me! I was given fifty dollars each from my grandparents and my parents to choose something I wanted from Disney. I was so excited, as I had been looking for a number of years for a glass globe with Cinderella's castle in it that plays the song, *Wish upon a star.*

My family and I looked all day for this globe while we were at Disney and it wasn't until we were walking out of the park down Main Street that Chris spotted it, all lit up in a shop window. It looked so beautiful and delicate with its dark wood base and glass globe. I was thrilled that he found it. He also found some other little gifts that he thought some of his friends would want. I remember that he spent all his vacation money on other people. While picking gifts out, Chris explained to me the meaning behind each and to whom each one was for. It was again, a true fairy tale. There was no better way to end our vacation than to be celebrating my birthday with family.

A New Awakening

"In the coldest February, as in every other month in every other year, the best thing to hold onto in this world is each other."
~ Linda Ellerbee ~

The time we leave Florida has always varied. Sometimes we wake up a little after midnight and are home late that evening, or we will leave in the late afternoon and make it home by the next midday. This particular year, 2000, we left around one in the afternoon. It's about a nineteen-hour trip without traffic, so that would put us home around eight or nine in the morning. I couldn't wait to get home and tell my friends all about my trip, plus it was my birthday at the end of the week and I was excited to have a party. Although I was excited to get back home, it was hard to leave such warm, sunny weather and return to a cold February in New York.

We stopped for dinner along the way, as well as for the rest rooms, and then Dad gave us our sleeping bags to wrap around us when we fell asleep. Everyone went to the bathroom except for me. I didn't have to go, so I waited in the van. Because we were coming from the south, we were all dressed for the warm weather, but by the time we got halfway home, it was fairly cold. We continued on our way and in the middle of the night, while Dad was still driving, I woke up because I was too cold.

I took off my seat belt to change into pants and, normally at that point, I would have either left my seat belt off or put it on really loose because I was sleeping, but I didn't. At first, I put my seat belt back on and settled down to my left, against Matt, who was in his car seat, but for whatever reason I felt that wasn't good enough. I had pulled my belt so tight that it hurt me to lie on the side of Matt's car seat so I just tried falling asleep with my head straight back. It was rather uncomfortable as I was not used to sleeping in the car that way, and I had no idea why I chose to keep that uncomfortable position to sleep in. I took notice of Anna and Chris who were fast asleep on the backbench of the van, as well as Mom in the front passenger seat.

At around three o'clock in the morning, I was awakened by a loud crash. I opened my eyes and all I could see was the color red. I couldn't get myself oriented and I felt like I was being tossed around in circles. Bursting the silence in the car, I heard screams from the backbench. I heard Chris call out my name. It was a cry, a scream that nobody likes to hear; a sound that never has a good outcome. I tried to turn my head to get to my siblings but I just could not do it. I had no idea what was going on and I began to panic.

Chaos

"Chaos results when the world changes faster than people."
~Unknown Author~

In a matter of seconds, the red blur had come to a halt. I realized that the red I was seeing was the interior of our van. There was what looked like powdered smoke everywhere I turned. I looked straightforward and saw the airbag had deployed in the driver seat. The smell of whatever came out of it was terrible; it made me sick to my stomach and I found it hard to breathe. I oriented myself long enough to see that we had landed upright, all four wheels on the ground. I was still in my seatbelt when I saw Dad jump out of the van and tell Mom to get out right away. When they were both out, he immediately realized we were all still in the van. I heard him scream out, "My babies, my babies!" He climbed back in the driver seat and reached back to unbuckle me and then Matt in his car seat next to me.

Dad told me to get out but the first thing I did was look behind me to find Anna and Chris, who had screamed my name. There were no signs of my siblings in the back row and I immediately told Dad they weren't there. I got out through the opening of the sliding door on the right hand side of the van; the door was no longer there. I stepped out into the dark with no shoes on and could barely walk. My right knee had popped out and was very swollen. I could say that I did something terrible to it, but I had just been in a small skiing incident a month earlier that put me on crunches. The week we went to Florida had been the first week I was off them. Whatever happened to my knee in the van made it much worse.

I couldn't walk. The ground was wet from a light mist and as soon as I moved my abdomen started hurting. I immediately wrapped my arms around my stomach and bent over, trying to breathe. My mom was standing right in front of me, as was some bearded man. He asked my mom if I was okay. She looked at him, then looked at me and screamed out, "She can't breathe, what do you think?" He followed with something that I cannot remember then said he was going to get help. I watched him run off to the front driver side of a blue van, directly in front of ours on the left hand side of the three-lane highway. We were located right before an overpass bridge.

I turned my head back towards our van and could not believe what I was looking at. Our family van did not look like a van anymore. It was now a piece of metal lying on the road. The sliding door and all the windows were gone, and because of the air bag going off, the inside of the van looked like someone had thrown a smoke bomb inside. The back of the van was completely smashed in, all the way up to the backbench. All of our belongings, sleeping bags, suitcases, CDs, Florida oranges, and everything else were all over the highway as if we had decided to camp out there. There was no spot on the road that wasn't covered in glass; it was everywhere. It seemed like there were people all over but I couldn't focus on any one person. I knew that man by the blue van had gone for help. I turned to look if he had called, but he had disappeared. *Did he call for help; did he just abandon us, who'll call for help now?* I wondered.

Over Here

"When we are no longer able to change a situation,
we are challenged to change ourselves."
~ Victor Frankl ~

I was just standing there with Mom, who was looking around screaming out for Chris and Anna. I was so scared that we couldn't find them; neither was answering. Dad brought Matt, who was moving ever so slightly, over to us. I thought he was dying or had hit his head really hard. He just looked so limp. Maybe it was because we were all sleeping and he hadn't quite woken up yet, he was only five. I couldn't understand how anyone could still be sleepy through all that though, which made me think something was probably terribly wrong.

Mom was holding him in her arms on the ground and I noticed his head and left arm were bleeding. I told Mom and she asked me to run back to the van and get something to wrap around his arm. I limped back in my socks and looked around inside the van. The only thing I could find was his security blanket he called, Dee dee. Dee dee went everywhere with Matt and was very special to him. When I brought it back to Mom she yelled at me for getting the blanket that he sleeps with. "Why would you get that? We can't use that, he loves his Dee dee!" she said to me. She caught me off guard when she said that; *Mom is a nurse*, I thought, *what is wrong with her?* I looked at her and then at Matt and replied, "Mom, he's bleeding very badly and this is the only thing we have…we have to use it." She used it but the look on her face made me want to cry. It was one of those looks where I just knew it broke her heart to do it but was forced to with no other option. I watched Mom wrap it around his arm and pull him in closer to her.

Soon after Mom wrapped his arm, two people on the top of the overpass bridge had shouted down, "I saw the whole thing, the guy ran that way." Dad shouted back, "You did? Find him, get him!" he yelled and then continued to look for Anna and Chris. I watched the two people run away from the bridge towards the direction they said the man had run. Dad was running around looking for Anna and Chris when from across the road, on the right-hand side, I hear my sister yell, "Daddy!" I looked over to her and she was standing on the other side of the guardrail towards the trees. My first thought was, *how did she get way over there and how is she standing?* Dad ran over to her, picked her up and brought her over to us.

At that point, there were too many people to count looking for my brother, Christopher, and all the paramedics and firemen had arrived. There were flashing lights everywhere. I didn't know who to pay attention to and I was getting very cold. Another very nice man came up to Anna and me, saying very calmly and soothingly that he was the one who had called for help and that he was going to pick me up to take me to a policeman because I didn't have shoes on. I thought I was going crazy because this was not the same man who said he was going to call for help earlier. I looked for that man again and I just did not see him. Right before he picked me up, I heard someone yell, "Over here!" A group of people ran to that area in the woods on the right-hand side of the road. They had found my brother.

It Will Be Okay, Right?

"Sometimes we love with nothing more than hope.
Sometimes we cry with everything except tears."
~ Gregory David Roberts ~

I was being carried over to a police car with Anna when I heard my mom yell over to my dad and the group of people by my brother. She told them very firmly not to move him until paramedics got to him. The man who was carrying Anna and me put us in the backseat of a cop car and I didn't understand why we were being locked back there with nobody to talk to or ask questions. Anna was nine at the time and she kept asking me if everyone was okay. I tried as hard as I could to stop shaking so I could try to help her stop shaking but my body had taken complete control over my mind. There was no stopping the shock my body was feeling. I wanted to calm her down somehow and told her to take a long, deep breath; everything would be okay. It had to be okay, right? I mean, we hadn't done anything wrong, we were just coming home from vacation.

As soon as I told Anna that everything would be okay, I thought of all the situations in which I had been worried that things wouldn't be okay with my siblings but they had turned out just fine. I remembered two occasions where Chris hit the front of his head pretty badly to the point where he had severe internal bleeding against the brain. He spent days in the hospital and everything was just "all better" when he came home. I hadn't understood how bad his injuries were until I was older.

My thoughts were interrupted as I watched the paramedics roll Chris out from the woods on a stretcher and put him into the back of an ambulance. They shut the doors and drove off quickly with the sirens on. I knew it wasn't good but kept telling myself everything would be okay. Someone finally came over to us and took us out of the police car. They asked us if we thought we could walk over to the ambulance. I did my best but it hurt to walk.

One of the paramedics asked me to lie down on one of the backboards; I had never been on one before. The paramedic team put a neck brace on me and strapped me to the board. I let them do their job but I just wanted to sit up so Anna could see my face. She was really nervous and began profusely shaking. As they did the same to Anna, I said to her, "Let everyone do what they have to, I'm lying right next to you." She quietly listened and shook slightly less than she had been. The paramedics were very friendly and they did make the ride feel less like the worst ride ever. They asked all kinds of random questions like our favorite colors and what we liked to do for fun. One of them did a really good job at distracting me until he asked me where we were coming from.

"We were on our way back home from Florida," I told the paramedic. That immediately got me back on track and I wanted to know everything; *where were my brothers and how come one of my parents wasn't with us*, I kept thinking, but he kept right on asking me questions that I thought were irrelevant to how I was feeling. "Did you go to Disney?" was his last question. I was angry with Disney right then. It was a happy memory that I really didn't feel like thinking about. It wasn't that Disney caused this accident but our fairy tale vacation was not supposed to end this way and I couldn't help but resent Disney at that moment. How could this perfect, innocent vacation end in such an opposite way of what everything Disney stands for, happy endings? I changed the subject on the paramedic and reversed the questions.

"Where are my brothers?" I asked the paramedic. He looked at me and waited a few seconds to answer; he seemed unsure of whether he should tell me or not. I was then told that one of my brothers was taken to a different hospital than the one we were going to because they could care for him better there and my other brother was in critical condition, already at the hospital. I asked the next logical question I could think of. Where were we?

Deep Breath

"I think people that have a brother or sister don't realize how lucky they are. Sure, they fight a lot, but to know that there's always somebody there, somebody that's family."
~ Trey Parker ~

"We are taking you to University Hospital in Baltimore, Maryland," another paramedic responded. *Maryland?* I thought. *How did we get so far in the trip, we were so close to home.* Well, compared to the length of the entire trip we were close; out of a nineteen-hour trip, we were only four hours away from home. One of them mentioned the time and date in recording information; it was around four o'clock in the morning on Sunday, February 27th. The ambulance pulled up to the hospital and Anna started to shake even harder when they pulled us out. I told her that everything would be okay, and watched out of the corner of my eye as the paramedic wheeled her away from me. I had this dreadful feeling that I wasn't going to see my family soon, maybe not ever again.

I was rolled into a very small, tight ER room and the paramedics left me there. I waited alone for what seemed like half an hour, still on the backboard with a neck brace on. I couldn't understand why everyone had left me, and why I hadn't heard anything about my parents. Questions and thoughts were racing through my head. I couldn't see anything, I couldn't move, and the only thing I could hear was the clock in the room ticking. It made time go by even slower. Dad finally walked in and sat down in the chair on the left side of my bed. I was instantly relieved to see that at least one family member was standing, walking in front of me, alive. I couldn't really move my head to look at him, but I could see him out of the corner of my eye. He began to tell me everything that had happened.

He took a deep breath, sighed, and teared up. He began by telling me that we were hit by a drunk driver, who then ran from the scene and the police were looking for him. "We are all in different places," he explained, and then told me where everyone was and why. Mom was only a few rooms down and was still on her backboard too. He told me the doctors were worried that she might have broken her neck. Anna, he said, was in the children's wing, doing okay but suffering from severe shock.

He went on to Matt next, who was taken to Johns Hopkins Hospital because he needed special care. Matt's left arm had been cut by the window glass that fell on him while he was sleeping. He was cut from his palm to his elbow on his anterior left forearm and Dad told me he might need skin grafting to repair it. Chris, he said, was in very critical condition with severe internal bleeding. That was all Dad knew about him at that time because he wasn't given any more information. I asked if Chris would be okay and Dad said, "I don't know Michelle, it's not good."

Dad got up and walked over to my side. He grabbed my hand, squeezed it and told me I would be okay. He went to sit with Mom and I was by myself again. Being by myself earlier had felt like an eternity, but after Dad gave me all that information then left, the next twenty minutes of solitude felt even longer. I felt extremely alone and all I wanted to know was if the rest of my family would be just as okay as Dad seemed to be.

A doctor finally came in with a team of nurses and cleared my neck brace and backboard. They took me off it and rolled me down several hallways to have MRIs and CAT scans. I had never had any of these tests before so I was clueless as to what I had to do. I left my earrings on and I didn't know I was supposed to take them off while having the testing. I felt so uncomfortable when the imaging technician snapped at me saying, "Don't you know you can't wear jewelry in these machines, now I'll have to do it again." I felt all alone and I so desperately wanted my family. I just wanted someone who loved me, who cared, sitting next to me so I knew I would be okay. And what about the rest of my family? I wouldn't be "okay" until I knew that everyone else was okay. The thought repeated over and over in my head, *what about my family? What about my family?*

Silently Waiting

"Silence is the most powerful scream."
-Author Unknown-

I was put in a wheelchair and taken down another hallway. I assumed that everything was okay with me. I wasn't put in a room because, I thought, we were just waiting for my parents to meet up with me. I didn't know where we were going but around the corner came Mom in a wheelchair with Dad walking next to her. She looked very tired but I was relieved to see that they were both okay. It didn't matter where we were going now because I was with my family. We were escorted to what looked like a lounge for people who were waiting to hear about loved ones. I remember the hospital being so big that the nurses escorting us barely knew where they were going.

The waiting room was on the right-hand side of the hallway and I don't think I have ever felt anything like the way I did when I was wheeled into that room. Inside, several nurses and doctors were sitting in a circle with their scrubs on. The nurses that brought us into the room added us to the circle, then left immediately. It was extremely quiet, too quiet for anything to be good. A pin, if dropped, would have sounded like a drawer of silverware hitting the ground. The sounds outside of the room felt magnified because there simply wasn't a sound within the four walls where we sat. I sat there as I went back and forth, very intently, between my parents' faces and the doctors' faces. One of the doctors finally began to speak, stuttering a little bit. He was explaining what the surgical team had been working on.

The doctor began by saying, "Your son, Christopher, we went in and tried operating; he had extensive internal injuries," he paused. I thought to myself, *what do you mean you 'tried'?* He went on saying, "We did everything we could but…he didn't make it." I stared at the doctor, waiting for a further response. Maybe his heart stopped and they got it going again is what he actually means. There was no further response. It was final. It was as if, in that moment, all forms of light were blown out or turned off and the world ceased from spinning. The words resonated in my head; he didn't make it, he didn't make it.

He…didn't…make it…

Giving Peace

"Blessed is the influence of one true, loving human soul to another."
~ George Eliot ~

At that moment, I watched my parents fall apart emotionally. I didn't know what to do. What are you suppose to do when you get news like that? Mom was uncontrollably crying with small gasps in between breaths. Dad had just gone to his knees with his head in his hands. I sat there thinking, *I am just a child, sitting here with my parents who are inconsolable. What am I suppose to say, how do I help?*

One of the first things my mom said while continuing to cry was, "Is anyone in here Christian?" I hadn't really expected anyone to come forward. I had this stereotype in my head that most people in the medical field did not believe in any religion, even though my mom and various other family members are in the medical field themselves. To my surprise, several raised their hands and Mom asked if they would pray with her. One of the female nurses said the prayer and my mom added on towards the end.

The head doctor asked my parents if they wanted to see my brother one last time. My mom very quickly said, "No, that is not my son anymore," and Dad just shook his head no. The doctor looked at me, awaiting my reply. I said no as well, because my parents said no. The very second I said it, I knew I didn't mean it. I had just said it because Mom and Dad said no and I thought there was something wrong in wanting to see him. Not looking at my brother is, by far, my biggest regret in life. I wanted so badly to look and be able to say goodbye. I didn't have the courage or strength to say I changed my mind and so watched the team of doctors walk out solemnly with their heads down.

I don't remember crying in that room while everyone was there. I just sat there staring at everything and everyone around me. Dad came over to me, on his knees, crying and told me it was okay to cry. I felt like I had broken down inside but it just wasn't showing on the outside. He put his head on my lap; I felt like I was in another world. I could physically feel his pain and anger slightly rising and, in that moment, the very first thing I thought of to say to him was a story he had told me just a month earlier. How coincidental it felt just hearing this story and having to retell it as it applied to our own lives now. It was a story from the Bible that fascinated and intrigued me much more than most of the others I had heard. It was the story of Job. I found it so profound that no matter what terrible things happened to this human being, his faith in God remained strong, despite others telling him to curse and hate God.

For those who don't know the story, it is about a man, called Job, who praises and believes wholeheartedly in God. The devil tries telling God that he can persuade even His most loyal followers to falter in their faith, because their love for Him (God) is not that strong. God allows the devil to try to persuade Job away from his faith with various different pains and illnesses. The devil took away his wife, children, home, and fields and made him very ill. Through each painful event, Job never cursed God. He didn't understand why God was allowing this to happen but he never cursed him. Job helped God prove the devil wrong and for that, he was rewarded tenfold.

I briefly brought this up to my dad. "Oh yeah," he said with a somewhat lightened voice. I could see the change in his face; it was as if he had found just the faintest inkling of peace. I don't know why that story came to mind almost immediately, but it did. And I don't know why I chose to remind him right at that moment, but if there could have been anything that helped him right then and there, that seemed to be it.

A Single Tear

"Tears are the silent language of grief."
-Voltaire -

I continued to sit in the lounge while my parents stepped out to the front desk. I could see them through the doorway, standing there by the phone. It was now around eight that Sunday morning and Dad was making phone calls to whomever he felt necessary right at that moment. He called our pastor, who would inform the church in only a few hours of what had happened. My grandparents from Florida were called, as well as my Aunt Jane who is Chris' godmother and one of my mom's sisters.

I think I was still taking in the words "he didn't make it" because I hadn't moved from my spot. I just couldn't move, as if by holding still another scenario would take the place of the one I didn't want. Chris was always a fighter; all those times he hit his head and he came back from it. What was the problem now? Why couldn't he be his stubborn self and push harder? And why wasn't I able to cry like I wanted to? I closed my eyes and watched the whole thing play over again underneath my eyelids. There must have been something I could have done to prevent it.

Dad came back over to me and touched my shoulder lightly. He told me that he and Mom were going to see Anna and that I should keep resting. *Right here, in the lounge,* I thought, *where people can come in and out watching me?* I normally would have gotten up and went with them despite what I was really feeling, tired. I had no energy to speak and I just didn't care about anything. I nodded and closed my eyes again.

Nobody was in the waiting room and I started talking to Chris at a whisper. I began with, "I don't know where you are right at the moment or what you are doing right now but this is not a funny joke. You are coming back, right? God will send you back to us because we love you, right?" I just knew I was wrong as soon as I said it. How could he be coming back? Death is permanent. I continued talking, "I don't know what happened, Chris. I'm so sorry I couldn't help you. I tried so hard to turn my head back to you. Please forgive me, please. I love you and I'll miss you more than anyone will know." As I spoke with my eyes closed, I felt a tear come down my left cheek. I just let the warm, wet tear stream all the way down my face and drop to the floor. I opened and closed my eyes a few times and quickly fell into a deep sleep.

Stupid Coloring Book

"Telling a teenager the facts of life is like giving a fish a bath."
- Arnold H. Glasow -

Someone woke me up. I can't remember if Mom or Dad came back to get me or if a nurse helped me down to my sisters room. Either way, my memory had become chaotic and choppy. I remember walking through her door and seeing her lying in the bed with a hospital gown on. Just looking at her, I could tell she already knew about Chris. I used my crutches and sat next to her bed. The first thing she said to me was, "They ripped my Mickey sweatshirt," and she gave me a pout face. I felt so terrible and I honestly did not know what to say to her.

Mom had explained to me that Anna had been throwing up all morning. The doctor thought it was just from shock, but they were going to keep her just to make sure she didn't have any internal bleeding. Anna's room was where we found out what happened to the man who hit us. A cop came in and explained to us that they took out dogs to find the man and ended up finding him lying in a field not too far from the accident scene. He was currently in the same hospital as us. I watched my dad take a deep breath.

The officer was so nice and was willing to answer any questions that any of us had. He explained where our van was and that someone was going to have to go and gather our things, but that the van was totaled. When the officer was getting ready to leave, a nurse came in to start discharging Anna. I wondered where we were going to go and how, without a car. My parents had said we would take a cab over to where Matt was in Johns

Hopkins Hospital. I hadn't heard too much about Matt other than that he was in that hospital, so I was worried that he wouldn't be okay.

In tragedy and traumatic events, the mind just simply cannot hold every single memory, let alone in sequential order. My memory now begins to skip between events and the next thing I remember is eating hospital food in a really small conference room with only one long table. A nurse brought my parents, Anna and I, fried chicken and mashed potatoes. Dad wouldn't even look at his food and when I smelled it, I felt nauseous. Someone came in with coloring books that were all about grief and gave them to Anna and me. The lady told me I could use it whenever I wanted or not at all, but it was for me to do what I wanted with it. I was quite offended that she categorized me with my nine-year-old sister and gave me, a fourteen-year-old, a coloring book. I looked at my dad, hoping he would chime in, but he was on the other side of the table, leaning back in the chair with his eyes closed. I began thinking to myself, *I know I'm not an adult but I just had to sit in a room with my inconsolable parents and did my best to bring comfort. How could anyone categorize me as a child? As someone who colored in grief workbooks?* If ever there were a time I should no longer be considered a child, this was it…after what I just went through. Only, I had no idea that this was just skimming the surface of the challenges that would be put in front of me. Adult in mind, a child in soul.

Asking me if I wanted a coloring book left such an impression on me that I don't remember much else from those hours other than being helped into a cab outside of the hospital. Dad helped me put my crutches in and Anna, Mom, and I got into the back while Dad sat up front. I was still thinking about how someone gave *me* a coloring book, what were these people thinking?

Strength of a Child

"Anyone can give up, it's the easiest thing in the world to do. But to hold it together when everyone else would understand if you fell apart, that's true strength."
~ Author Unknown ~

It was still Sunday, February 27th but in the afternoon, and we were going into Matt's hospital room. I was a little afraid to see him because I didn't know what condition he'd be in, as I hadn't heard anything about him other than the fact that he was in this particular hospital. All of us walked in his room, me being the last one to enter in fear that there would be more trauma that I'd have to see. I was surprised to see my little five-year-old brother sitting up in this huge bed with my Aunt Jane beside him, keeping him company. The bed was in the middle of the room on the left side, so walking into the room, Matt in his bed was the first thing I could see.

Aunt Jane saw us and immediately stood up. With pain in her face and tears in her eyes, she walked towards my mom and held her in her arms. It was so hard for me to watch the people I cared most about be in so much pain, knowing I couldn't do anything about it. Once everyone sat back down, I really got to see how Matt was doing. His little left arm was completely bandaged with a white board underneath it to keep it from moving too much. He looked so tired, but relieved to have his family around him.

Because we had all walked in together, I knew that Matt had no idea about our brother, Chris, and I would have to hear someone tell him what happened. It might have been easier if I had been in the room with Anna when Mom and Dad told her; it would have given me some experience to go on. The topic seemed to be avoided for quite some time, with different things, like what was on his TV or how nice his room looked with bright colors and cute animal figures around on the walls. It didn't take too long for Matt to realize that Chris wasn't around and he wanted to know where he was.

Matt looked around the room, then at Mom and Dad, and we knew what was coming. "Where is Chris?" he asked the room. The room fell completely silent as everyone looked at each other, wondering who else besides themselves would be the one to tell him what happened and "where" Chris was. As soon as he asked, my heart fell and I could just feel the hurt collecting inside of my chest.

Dad opened his mouth as if he were going to speak, and just sighed. He stood up from his chair, in the farthest corner of the room towards the foot of the bed, and walked over to Matt to sit in the chair closest to him. He put his elbows on the side of the bed and gently touched Matt's upper arm. I could see the fear and pain already surfacing in Matt's face in anticipation of what Dad was going to tell him, yet his body seemed so calm and relaxed. Dad began, "Chris." He paused with tears in his eyes, then continued, "Chris is in Heaven now." I had expected my little brother to break down in tears or ask more questions. His reaction took me by surprise and made it more painful for me to watch him try to be strong. Matt just stared silently at Dad and replied with a simple, meek "Okay," as he put his head down, looked back up, and straightened his posture.

The Need to Escape

"We all try to escape pain and death, while we seek what is pleasant."
- Albert Einstein -

How could God allow this little, innocent boy to experience so much pain? It absolutely killed me to watch my brother "suck it up" and try to be brave. I had to turn around and face the door while I recomposed myself before I could look at him again. Although I had responded in nearly the same way, of not crying, it broke my heart that he was forced to grow up well beyond a five-year-old's emotional capabilities within a matter of hours. The same goes for my sister. I hadn't really been concentrating on my pain, but on theirs, and how unfair it was. If it were at all possible, I would have taken all of my family's pain in that one little hospital room and beared it upon myself.

There was pain everywhere. I just didn't know where to begin or where to go from this point, now that everyone in my immediate family knew exactly what happened. People were coming in and out of his room like it was a fast food restaurant, each for different reasons. One nurse was coming in to take his blood, another checking his vitals and a third changing the wraps on his left arm that had the cuts. There were cops coming in and out asking questions and giving updates as to what was going on with our van, the man who hit us and what my parents had to do next as far as legal action.

It was still Sunday afternoon, but it felt like days had gone by. In part, I'm sure, because I had been sitting in this one room all day after coming from the University

Hospital. I wanted to move, leave, get out of the area. I was extremely restless. Having people come in and out wasn't helping the feeling either. *What if I just walked out with the next person leaving?* I thought to myself. I thought I might have a change in scenery when one of the policemen had said someone needed to go to where the van was and collect all the things we wanted, and throw away all the unsalvageable belongings.

My parents said they didn't want to see the van at all so Aunt Jane offered to go and rummage through everything. I wanted to go so badly. "Can I go with her, Dad?" I got the courage to ask. "No, I don't think so," was his reply. I was disappointed because I wanted to see what happened to the van without being in shock or smack in the middle of all the chaos. I felt like I needed to process what happened to us by looking at the product of it all; I was curious. I'm positive the reason why Dad told me no was only to protect me from pain and more shock, but it bothered me at the time. I may not have been an adult to them but I was old enough to know what I wanted to process for myself.

If I couldn't go with her, then I was going to come up with whatever I could think of that I had in the van and knew I wanted back no matter what condition they were in. I had CDs in there and books from school, along with souvenirs I had bought. I immediately thought of the glass Disney globe that Chris found for me and wanted it desperately. I was afraid if it was broken nobody would give it to me in fear that it would bring a lot of pain. I didn't care, I had to see it. I wanted to know what happened to my things. I knew now that seeing my brother, Chris, in the hospital would never happen, so I clung to whatever I could that would remind me of him. Sure enough, Mom and Dad had made it clear that they thought all glass objects were broken and told me not to have my hopes up.

I was getting agitated and glad that my Aunt was on her way out which would end the conversation. I just didn't care to discuss this anymore. After she left, we had a visitor.

Unbreakable Gift

"Give what you have. To someone it may be better than you dare to think."
~ Henry Wadsworth Longfellow ~

There were so many people who came to visit us, some of them I didn't know, and others who were familiar and whose presence comforted me. This particular visitor I hadn't known other than the memory I had of him carrying Anna and I to the police car. He was very kind and gave us his condolences. He explained to my dad, with a heavy heart, what he had seen from the accident and then began to share with us how he lost his brother on the same road in an accident. "This road is terrible, so many accidents happen right around here," he went on to explain. I'm not sure this comment helped the situation or made it worse.

I didn't know him and he didn't really know us but I felt some sort of connection in the fact that he lost his brother too. He wasn't at all near my age. In fact, he was more than double my age, with me being fourteen, but it was still comforting to know that my siblings and I weren't the only ones in the world at that moment that had lost a sibling. Right before he left, he gave my family his information and said, "If you ever need anything and I can help, please let me know."

Not too long after he left, Aunt Jane returned with what she could in her car. I sat on the edge of my seat with my heart racing, waiting to hear whether she found my globe, and if she had actually brought it back. It was as if she read my mind because I didn't even have to ask. With a slight smile on her face, she said, "It's one of the only glass things I found untouched." I was relieved and, to be honest, quite surprised; those globes are very easily broken. The globe then became the last "gift" that I would always remember from my brother.

Regain a Sense of the World

"Reality is too much to take in heapfuls, but sprinkle it sparingly upon life's path and most can tread it lightly."
~ Astrid Alauda ~

We stayed in Matt's room for a few more hours and Aunt Jane took Anna and me to the nearest Ronald McDonald house. I had no idea what this place was, so when she told me where we were going, the first thing I thought of was, *We're sleeping at a McDonald's?* As we were walking to Aunt Jane's car on the top lot level, she explained to me what it was; "It's like a hotel for people who need a place to stay when a loved one is in need of care far from home."

It felt so good to get up and walk out of the hospital. I was stepping out of my life for a few hours to possibly regain a sense of the world. My own reality had been too much for me to take in, in those short hours, and I needed others' reality, the commonality of what goes on in the world on a daily basis, to help balance me out. Walking with Anna and Aunt Jane to her car was the first time all day that I had felt someone was really paying attention to me. She wanted to know how we were feeling and if there was anything she could get us. I didn't feel bombarded with questions or overwhelming pain, it was just enough to feel consoled; my family was here. I felt safe; that warm feeling you get when someone you just *know* would do anything for you, and surrounds you with this force field of protection called love.

I don't remember much from being at the Ronald McDonald house other than knowing who got which bed for the night, helping Anna, and checking out in the morning. Anna had brush marks on her back that needed to be cleaned and tended to each night. Aunt Jane took off Anna's gauze and gently cleaned it while talking to her with a calm voice. None of us knew what caused her small wounds, but for being tossed out of a moving van, thrown across a major highway and landing in the woods on the other side of the guard rail, it was a wonder how that's all she got, and nothing short of a miracle.

I remember the Ronald McDonald house as being a place for me to become numb, a place where the pain no longer existed. The times that I remember being numb are the times I cannot recall as well as the other memories. I don't really know what happens to your brain and body when becoming numb, whether the memory is just repressed so far back that it's harder to retrieve or whether the body automatically chooses to forget those traumatic memories in an effort to protect itself. Either way, I wish there was some way I could get all of my memory back.

The next morning, Aunt Jane checked us out and we went back to the hospital to be with Matt, Mom and Dad.

Life Backwards

"Some laugh, while others mourn;
Some toil, while others pray;
One dies, and one is born: so runs the world away."
~ Samuel Wesley ~

It was now February 28th, and time couldn't have passed more slowly. It seemed like I had been there for a year. This day was the busiest one that I remember in the hospital, not the most chaotic but the busiest. Matt's room still looked the same with all the little animals lining the wall and the machines beeping every few seconds. We had so many people that we knew come see us. I couldn't keep track of who was coming and who was going and I couldn't tell you who came first and who came last but I remember distinctly each person that came.

When we arrived back to his room, family friends that live in Maryland were there. Growing up, we rarely got to see this family but it was always a fun time when we did. Mom explained to me when I was little that in Maryland, instead of calling someone Mrs. Smith or Mr. Smith, they call each other Ms. Anna or Mr. Matt. Ms. Rose and Mr. Dan is how I knew them and will always know them. Mr. Dan was playing Old Maid with Matt when we walked in, while Ms. Rose was talking with Mom. Ms. Rose and my mom had gone to college together in Maryland, keeping in touch throughout the years.

Ms. Rose didn't have to say anything to express how she was feeling; the pain written on her face was enough. The one thing she said that sticks out in my mind was when she was explaining how she found out.

Our accident had happened only minutes from her house and she heard it on the news that morning. I remember her saying, "I was listening to the news and felt for the family because that road is terrible, but never did I ever imagine that it would be one of my best friends." Everybody knew we would be in Maryland for at least another day and so she offered her house for anyone to come and stay. My eyes widened when she offered. *It would be so nice to stay in a familiar place*, I thought. I accepted the offer without hesitation and Anna decided to come along as well. They both left and would come back sometime later in the day to pick us both up.

My grandparents got there during the day, as they drove up from Florida as soon as they received the call. I saw them pass Matt's hospital room as they were looking for us, so Mom got up to find them. Just before Mom left my sight, they found each other in the doorway. I watched as my mom engulfed herself in her own mother's arms and just fell apart crying, saying, "My son, my baby." All three of them stood there crying as I watched from inside the room.

Watching everybody else's pain manifest itself so intensely, hurt me tremendously. I knew it was hurting that terribly because I had never seen my family this badly hurt, and they rarely cried. I was fourteen, watching the process of life work backwards. My grandparents should never have had to watch their child lose a child and my parents should never have had to lose a child or watch any of their children suffer such a loss. Yet the idea of death surrounded us, life continued to go on in this room, in a much different way, whether we wanted it to or not. In fact, life would move onward everywhere and the world still turned despite the feeling that my entire world had come to a dead halt in that hospital room. Life went on.

You Didn't Know

"Guilt is perhaps the most painful companion of death."
~ Coco Chanel ~

Not remembering the order of when people came makes my memories a little more confusing, although while the visitors were there I can remember the time quite vividly. Other than Aunt Jane, my grandparents and my mom's friends from Maryland, I had not expected anybody else to come. If we were in New York, I wouldn't have been all that surprised to see people, being our home state, but Maryland was at least four hours away without traffic. I knew our situation was serious but it really hit me when people from New York drove all the way down to see us. This meant the world thought it was just as serious as I did and I would be in for many more chaotic and overwhelming experiences when I returned to New York.

Our pastor and his wife drove down to see us and spent quite some time in Matt's room. He explained that he informed the entire church, and everyone's hearts went out to us. He mentioned a few names of my friends from church that had specifically wanted me to know they asked further about me. If they hadn't mentioned my friends, I would have kept on forgetting that friends and people outside of this room even existed. I completely forgot that I had friends that were probably wondering what exactly happened and when they were going to talk to me.

Dad had co-workers that drove all the way down to see him. How compassionate, I thought, for these guys to take off work and drive to be with another co-worker. I remember sitting near enough to clearly listen to their conversation. I'm not sure if I was meant to hear it or whether Dad just didn't care at that point, but I found myself fascinated by the "adult" conversation they were having.

Dad was leaning up against the wall just outside of Matt's hospital room, with one of his friends standing diagonally next to him, holding his hand over his mouth and his eyebrows expressing deep thought. Dad explained his story and repeated it again and again. He said, "I just don't understand." He paused a moment. "I had literally just looked in the rearview mirror; if I had just looked up again and switched lanes." He went on with his "if only's" and I couldn't get over to him fast enough with my crutches before his friend stole the words right out of my mouth. "You didn't know; how could you?" I sat back down slowly without recognition. I was happy someone else shared my thoughts.

The next thing I remember, my sister and I were with Ms. Rose.

The Warmth of a Gentle Family

"Where there is peace, God is."
~ George Herbert ~

Ms. Rose was very good at distracting me from the reality I had been facing over the past twenty-four hours and some. She needed to go food shopping and brought us along with her, making appropriate jokes about different things here and there. On the car ride back to her house, she explained that her children's grandfather had passed away after being in a car accident as well and her son, Steven, would be especially upset to hear about what had happened to us. I liked the way she had phrased that; instead of saying she had lost her father-in-law, she related the loss from her children's perspective. It made me feel less alone, knowing that others around my age would know what it felt like to lose someone unexpectedly in an accident.

It was refreshing to be able to stay in a home, let alone the home of people I felt comfortable with. Walking into the house, I strung one bag of small groceries on my left crutch. It was fairly hard to walk with it but I felt obligated to do as much as I could, as she and her husband were so graciously letting my sister and I stay in their home. It felt so good being able to take a real shower and sit with a family for dinner. You would think that I hadn't had any of these things for weeks with the way I appreciated it. It certainly felt, at the time, like I hadn't had those things in weeks.

Mr. Dan, their son, Steven, and daughter, Megan, came home just before dinner and I thought I was going to have to explain everything that happened, in as much detail as I could remember because their kids would want to know. This was not the case; in fact, it turned out quite the opposite. Not once was I asked a single question about what happened, nor was the topic even brought up. I felt safe.

Age-wise, I am a year younger than Megan and a year older than Steven; Chris was a year younger than Steven. Seeing them, I was taken back to the times the four of us spent together playing downstairs in their basement or outside in their backyard and pool. Chris would always pal up with Steven and tease me about anything they could. Ms. Rose would always tell me that was Steven's way of telling me he liked me, which I apparently didn't understand because I thought grabbing hold of my neck, and trying to dunk me under water was a form of torture! When Steven saw me that afternoon, the look on his face was of pure disgust, not for me but for what had happened. Ms. Rose had been right. He shook his head and continued past me to his room. It was actually a relief that nobody asked questions or even mentioned the fact that we were in an accident.

Ms. Rose had been so kind to take care of the brush wounds on Anna's back and helped her take a bath. She took care of us both as if we were her own and I could think of no other place I'd rather have been in such a situation; I felt peace in their home. What would have happened if this took place in another state, someplace where nobody we knew had been close by? It was strangely ironic to have been hit exactly where we had been, only minutes from those who cared about us.

Sometime after dinner, I asked if I could make a phone call. I wanted to call one of my friends from home. Ms. Rose brought me to her room where it was quiet and gave me time to talk. Someone on the other end answered the phone and I immediately wanted to be in New York. I felt my emotions escalating as everyone in their family gathered around the phone saying, "It's Michelle." They each took turns asking me questions, "What happened?" "How are you doing?" and "Are you ok?" I wanted so badly to jump through the phone to be with them and, at the same time, I was a little overwhelmed with the questions and just wanted to hang up and go back to the peaceful, "normal" family life I was experiencing.

I briefly explained where everyone was and that I thought I would be home either tomorrow or the following day. I hung up and returned to the peaceful living room where everyone was watching TV. One by one everyone started getting up to go to bed and Steven and I were left alone.

I wasn't tired at all and thought I would be up the entire night watching TV on the couch. We hadn't really spoken to each other the entire night and then out of the silence Steven quietly said, "It's okay if you don't want to be alone. I'll sit here until whenever you fall asleep." I stared at him, looking straight into his eyes, thinking of what words to use other than "thank you" to express how grateful I was. I nodded my head in agreement, "Okay," I finally said, softly. It mattered to me that Steven stayed in the room. His presence alone brought a peaceful comfort and I was extremely thankful that he *wanted* to be there. I must have fallen asleep because I was then woken up by Megan, who helped me get to my bed. Her voice was so calm and her touch was gentle; I felt like I was dreaming.

Unexpected Interrogation

"Justice denied anywhere diminishes justice everywhere."
~ Martin Luther King Jr. ~

We were now back in Matt's hospital room with the rest of my family. It was Tuesday, February 29th, because of leap year. Things seemed to be wrapping up there as far as where each of my family members was going. Anna and I were going to be taken home by Grandma and Grandpa in their big GMC van, Aunt Jane would take Dad home and along the way take care of funeral arrangements. Matt had to be transported by helicopter back to New York so Mom was going to stay and fly back with him. While all these plans had just been finalized, a Maryland police officer on the scene of our accident came in to speak with Dad.

The officer came to make sure everything was taken care of and that there were no more immediate questions or concerns. I remember the cop asking Dad, as if the question had already been asked a few times and he was clarifying, "You didn't see the guy?" My ears perked up and I looked at Mom; nobody asked *me* about the guy and I was sure I had seen him with Mom around. My eyes went back and forth between Dad and the officer, waiting for someone to mention the fact that it was possible someone else could have seen him. I was too shy to speak up on my own in front of the cop and so waited until he was just leaving Matt's room to tell Dad.

"I saw him, Dad," I said quietly. I had expected him to calmly sit with me and ask questions while someone returned the officer to the room, but he took me by surprise when he raised his voice a few notches. "Why didn't you say anything before?" he asked with a little frustration in his tone. I put my head down. I wasn't sure I wanted to share anymore after a reaction like that. "You saw him too, Mom. Don't you remember?" I asked her. She stared blankly at me. She had no idea what I was talking about. When the officer returned, Dad explained to him that I thought I might have seen the guy. Because I had seen him, the officer explained that I needed to be questioned but that it wasn't necessary for me to come down to the station; he could bring all that was needed right to me.

Grandma and Grandpa were ready to go and Dad wasn't too happy that I had waited until so late in the afternoon to even mention my encounter with the man who hit us. We waited until the officer returned with a tape recorder and a picture line up of several men in jail. I had never had to do anything like this before, let alone have this much contact with a policeman. The most I had ever been involved with a cop was with my fifth grade D.A.R.E officer. This was far more frightening.

Mom stayed with me in the hospital room. I can't remember if anybody else was in the room or not, I was concentrating on what the officer was doing. He started out by telling us the process of testifying, being a witness and what would be recorded. The record button was pressed and he stated who was participating, either by speaking (myself) or being a witness to the testifying (my mom). I was then asked to explain what I remembered happening.

I very slowly shared what I remembered about the accident and the encounter I had with the man I thought might have hit us. He was the first person I saw when stepping out of the van, the man who had asked my mother if I was okay and would call for help. I stated that I watched him walk towards his van to call for help and when I turned my head for a minute, he was nowhere to be found.

The next question out of the officer's mouth proved to only me that I really had seen the man who hit us. "Were you holding your stomach when you got out of the van?" he asked me. I looked at him and asked in my head, H*ow did you know that?* I replied to him with a "Yes." The only reason the officer could have known that is if the man shared that piece of information with him. The officer asked me to choose one or more men from the picture line up that I thought was him or may look like him. I chose number one and that was the end of the interview. He said he'd be in touch with my dad. Did I really just do that? Did I really just sit through a line up and have to pick out the man who destroyed our family? The man who took my brother's life? I don't think I'll ever know how to describe the way I felt when I had to look at their faces, knowing one of them had killed my brother.

Buckingham Palace

"When you're safe at home you wish you were having an adventure; when you're having an adventure you wish you were safe at home."
~ Thornton Wilder ~

I was extremely nervous about the way the Maryland officer had left things. Why would he have to be in touch with Dad? Did I say the right or wrong thing and how long would we have to wait to hear back from him? I would have to wait patiently.

Grandma and Grandpa took Anna and me home in their huge GMC van. Nobody asked us if that would be okay or if we'd rather go in a different car. I suppose we didn't have any other choice. But if we did have a choice, going with Grandma and Grandpa couldn't have been a better decision. I just wanted to go home and hadn't really thought about the driving part. It didn't bother me to get back into a vehicle. Being in a car was just so much a part of everyday life that the accident hadn't fazed me to the point of not wanting to get into a car, despite what had happened. I don't think the ride would have been as smooth if I were in a smaller van or car, but because I was so high up, I felt that if anything were to happen, this big vehicle would protect me. On the down side, being in such a big vehicle and going around sharp turns made it feel like we were going to tip over. The bucket seats were so soft and comfortable; the best thing I could have done for myself at that moment was fall asleep and not pay attention to the road.

I remember crossing the George Washington Bridge and thinking there was roughly only an hour left and I would be home where it was quiet.

Home and my own room never sounded so good. When we pulled onto my street between 9 and 10 PM, it was dark, and most of all, the street was quiet. As soon as our house was in view, that feeling of quietness seemed to evaporate. I had expected the house to be dark looking, as our family had not been in it for over a week. I was wrong. There were several candles all over my front porch and lawn as well as cards and flowers of different types. The candles lit up the entire front of our house, causing us to be able to see everything else that was placed on the lawn. Normally, candles would give off a calm, relaxing feeling but at that moment, there were so many, it was just overwhelming and made me feel like people were everywhere. Arriving home made me realize this was as quiet as it would get for a long time. It was almost as if we had carried the loss, strapped to the top of the van, and brought it right into our driveway, into our home.

We walked inside, turned on the first light we came to and saw a living room filled with more cards, flowers and unlit candles. I thought the amount of gifts outside was a lot, I never imagined my living room being so filled that there was no more room for whatever was left outside. Could this really have been happening to me? My brother had only died two days ago and there was what looked like weeks of cards, flowers and candles on our property. One might have thought Princess Diana had just died and it was Buckingham Palace. Things were surely different at home and would be from now on, but I was home, *my* home, and that was all that mattered to me in those moments.

Someone had left a note on the kitchen table about the food that was made for us and kept warm in the oven. Our next-door neighbors and others who lived just a few houses down the road had been taking care of our dog for the week and now would be taking care of our whole family and house. My next-door neighbor, Frank, who is also Chris and my best friend, saw that we had arrived at home. He called and wanted to know if it would be okay to stop by before we all went to bed. We hadn't even begun to think about eating yet, so Grandma told him and his family to come on over. Frank would be the first person I saw after getting back home. I was anxious but scared to see him. What if neither of us knew what to say? How did he find out and what happened while I was in Maryland?

"Mourning" Was Inevitable

"To spare oneself from grief at all costs can be achieved only at the price of total detachment, which excludes the ability to experience happiness."
- Erich Fromm -

I have known Frank for as long as I have memory. His family moved next door to us when Frank and I were two years old. Whenever one family had a crisis the other one was right there making sure everything stayed on track. Both families thought the worst situations we would have to deal with had already passed and had been completely endured. All of us kids, including Frank and his younger sister Maryann, had our fair share of bumps, bruises, cuts, and stitches.

As kids, it didn't matter whether one of us needed stitches because a large tree branch fell on us or one of us was having a seizure while playing; we all *knew* that everyone would be okay. You go to the hospital, get the treatment/medicine needed and you come home good as new, usually with an extremely interesting story and a battle wound. What was I was going to say to Frank this time when he came in, knowing that this was not just a battle wound?

Frank and the rest of his family walked in and we were all in the kitchen beginning to partake in the heated chicken parmesan that one of our neighbors had made for us, still warm in the oven. I got up, made my way over to the front door, and asked if Frank wanted to sit down in the living room. As we walked over to my couch, candles and flowers surrounded us on all the living room tables, as well as on the floor and on top of our entertainment system. We sat there for a few minutes in silence until he said, "I still can't believe he's gone." I shook my head in agreement; "It's really real." I began telling Frank a little bit about what happened in Maryland and where the rest of my family was.

I was extremely interested to find out how things panned out here at home while we were all in Maryland, so I asked him everything I could think of. He explained that there were so many people at our house placing cards, candles and flowers, and there had even been a few news stations filming. "They were walking to different houses, trying to interview people about what happened and how they felt," Frank said. "It bothered me. It's a good thing you guys weren't here because you would have been bombarded by all of them."

Frank changed the topic slightly by explaining that the high school had a moment of silence and people were asking him about me. He asked when I would be coming back to school. We always walked to school together just about two blocks away. I hadn't really thought about not going to school and so replied quickly to his question with, "I'm going tomorrow." Frank looked at me, surprised and unsure if that's what I really wanted to do. I was sure. I did not want to be around anything of Chris' any more than I had to be and if school would take me away from the house, then that was what I was going to do. I wasn't ready to feel anything and I was comfortable with detaching myself from any emotion; being away from home would allow me to continue that. "See you in the morning," Frank said. He gave me a hug and went back home with his dad. I was nervous, but morning was inevitable.

Senora

"A little consideration, a little thought for others, makes all the difference."
- Winnie the Pooh -

My alarm clock went off at 6 AM on Wednesday March 1st, one day before my birthday. I was extremely tired and hit the snooze button. The alarm went off again, five minutes later, and it took everything I had to roll out of bed. I got myself ready and packed my school things; it took much longer with crutches.

Frank and I would walk to school together every morning since the first day of high school. We were now halfway through our freshman year. Frank would always come get me because my house was on the left side of his, along the way to school. We had a school bus but it was pointless for us to wait for it when we could be at school whenever we felt like it. I wasn't sure how walking was going to be with my crutches and my backpack but Frank was there to help.

We started walking past my house at 6: 30 AM, up the hill that we live on. The hill isn't too bad to walk up when you are fully capable, but it was a workout carrying my heavy backpack while on crutches. Frank kept asking me if I was okay, if I wanted him to go back and get one of his parents to drive us, but I kept pushing. I really did not know how to accept help. We got about halfway and a car drove by us, stopped, and reversed to meet us. It was our Spanish teacher.

Our Spanish teacher, whom we called Senora, was the first person that I knew and saw in public since our accident and I certainly was not prepared for it. She was one of our favorite teachers and always made things fun to learn. The car stopped, was put in park, and she stepped out with the most empathetic facial expression I had ever seen. She just stood there for a few seconds with her hand on her heart, her head tilted to the side and began to tear up. "Please, let me take you to school" she said. I looked at Frank for a response because students weren't allowed to get in cars with any teacher. "It's okay," he said. "It's not that far, we just need to cross the street."

She wanted to help in the worst way and seemed to have felt terrible that I was walking to school on crutches. She continued to plead with us, "Please, let me do this for you," she continued. I looked at Frank and nodded that it was okay. She and Frank helped me get in the back seat and she drove us across the main road, down the entranceway, and dropped us off in the front of the main entrance to the high school. Her response to me was so kind and motherly, but it definitely had me wondering if entering this school was the best idea. I got out of the car, took a deep breath, looked at Frank, who gave me a reassuring nod, and we walked inside the school.

Bodyguard

"A good friend is a connection to life – a tie to the past, a road to the future, the key to sanity in a totally insane world."
~ Lois Wyse ~

We were in school fairly early and I honestly didn't know what to expect with anything, although I certainly did not expect what did occur. I hadn't lost anybody in my life like this before. My grandpa on my dad's side had past away a few years prior but I was old enough to understand that "older people die first" so I was clueless as to how others would react to what happened to my family and me. All I knew was that my purpose for going to school was to get away from "my brother," his things and the chaos I knew would become of my home.

I don't remember who I saw first or even if there was a "first" person that I saw. I do remember being in a crowd of my friends standing all around me, silent. It seemed like the group got bigger and bigger, adding one to two people every few minutes. I'm not claustrophobic but I felt very strange being the center of attention for this type of occasion. I was use to dancing in the center of circles at parties and dances, but I wasn't comfortable with this type of attention. Frank was right by my side, like a bodyguard, ready to do whatever I needed. He was the closest thing I had to my brother at that moment and I found comfort in him never leaving my side.

I started walking on crutches towards my locker and the group of friends followed close around me as if I needed to be protected. I stood by my locker, grabbing the things I needed for my first class, with the halls starting to crowd up. I was fairly neutral with my emotions and nothing was really fazing me. I had become numb. People's eyes started to get glassy and some even shed a few tears, but I just wanted to continue my "normal" day.

As everyone around me was wiping their tears and putting their hands on my shoulder, a male peer whose locker was right next to mine looked at everyone and sarcastically said, "Why does everyone look like someone just died, who died?" Frank looked like one of those cartoon characters who just ate a hot pepper. He had lost his patience and temper rather quickly and told the guy, "Shut up before I knock you to the floor." I guess the guy really didn't know because he had asked again which agitated Frank even more. I stopped Frank from stepping closer to the guy and quietly answered his repeated question. "My brother died," I said and just walked away handing my books to the person standing next to me so I could use my crutches.

I was exhausted and I hadn't even gone to my first class. I walked down the freshmen hallway, again with Frank and friends walking behind me. I swear time went into slow motion as I started to walk. It was as if I was a movie star and everyone respectfully parted from the middle of the hall. All eyes were on me, and heads bowed as I passed, almost as if I were royalty. I had never seen or felt anything like it and could only imagine that I received a very small glimpse of what celebrities go through. Throughout the entire hallway, people in my grade were staring and repeatedly asking if I was okay. I answered "Yes," after "Yes," after "Yes" until I got to the end of the hallway where my class was.

Right before I entered the classroom on the right hand side, another male classmate again asked the same question, "Are you okay?" I had had it with the questions and the smothering. I just wanted to get to my class like a "normal," everyday teen. I snapped at him saying, "Do I look okay? I'm on crutches and my brother just died, what do you think?" I continued into the classroom without hesitation, with Frank by my side. As the words were spoken, it felt incredibly relieving, but the second the last syllable came out of my mouth, I immediately regretted it and was mortified I could act that way. I didn't have the courage or strength to go back out, face him and apologize.

Dictated Orders

"We can never turn back the pages of time, though we may wish to relive a happy moment, or say goodbye just one last time, we never can, because the sands of time continue to fall, and we can't turn the hourglass over."
~ Unknown Author ~

First period bell rang and I was sitting in earth science. I had a number of friends in this class sitting near me and that made it less awkward. The seating arrangement was set up like a horseshoe with two rows, so I was facing half the class. Everyone on the other side of the horseshoe stared at me, probably wondering what was going through my head or what I'd really been through; couldn't say I blamed them.

Our teacher got started right away, talking about water tables. I was still thinking about the words and tone of voice I had used just before coming to class. *How could I have said that and in that way?* I kept thinking. I didn't want him to think I was normally like that and began thinking of how I could apologize without making another scene. I had wished with all my thought power that I could go back in time and take it back, or for that matter, go back and prevent our accident, then I wouldn't be in this position in the first place. No matter how hard you wish, would like to, want, plead or pray with everything you've got, just to go back, life is not a video game, there are no re-do's, no check points to start from or gain an extra life; time only moves in one direction.

Everything went through my head besides the topic I should have been thinking about, water tables. I wondered what Frank was doing and if he was as restless as I was. I wanted him with me. What were all these people thinking that kept looking at me? I wasn't offended at all, I just knew they had questions on their minds and I wanted to know what they were. I had expected my teacher to talk with me or at least acknowledge me before class started. She hadn't, and began class as if it was just another day to her. Didn't she know it wasn't just another day? She never said anything to me that day nor ever.

In the middle of my thoughts, someone knocked on our classroom door and entered. It was the principal, who I had never met personally, asking to see me. I was quite shocked; *What did I do?* I thought. When people got pulled from classes by the principal it was usually for something they did or had been involved in. I think the class was just as surprised as I was because, as I grabbed my crutches and began walking, everyone looked at each other in puzzlement. This principal was one, we all knew, you didn't want to encounter even when you did nothing wrong. She didn't have the nicest demeanor and always looked like she was having an awful day.

My principal pulled me out of class to tell me that she wanted me to see my guidance counselor at some point just to touch base and maybe talk about what happened. I wasn't really too sure why she wanted me to do that and what was so urgent about this that she needed to take me out in the middle of class. It wasn't a suggestion or information for me to simply know it was there. It felt like an order, something I must do, especially after she said, "I'll be checking in with your counselor to make sure you've come." I returned to class even more agitated than I was when I first got there. This day was turning out to be a lot busier than I had expected or wanted and it had only just begun.

A Glimpse Of Comfort

"To ease another's heartache is to forget one's own."
~ Abraham Lincoln ~

The entire day at school people kept acknowledging the fact that I was there so soon and wondered why. I guess nobody expected me to be there for at least a few more days. I didn't feel like explaining myself over and over again so I just shrugged my shoulders whenever I heard anything along those lines.

I don't remember when I decided to go down to my guidance counselor's office but someone dropped me off there with my stuff. I was quite defensive about going. I thought I'd never need a counselor and now people were telling me I had to go. I sat down and my guidance counselor spun her chair around, with a beautiful smile on her face. "Hi, I'm Mrs. Reed. Are you Michelle?" I nodded and explained why I was there; the principal said I *had* to come. She smirked. "Well you didn't *have* to, it's not a requirement. I think she meant that I was here if you happened to want to talk."

I liked Mrs. Reed from the moment I walked in, even though I was rather defensive. She was upbeat, smiled a lot, and seemed down to earth. She's one of those exceptional people that you find who are absolutely beautiful both inside and out. I felt comfortable in her presence and her personality reminded me of an older version of myself. I wouldn't admit it there, in her office, but I knew I would be coming back to see her.

Our first encounter really didn't consist of very much and only lasted for about fifteen minutes, but it was something, an outlet I hadn't really known about. She understood me in saying that it must be overwhelming to come back to school with so many people looking and wondering what happened. Chris was never mentioned and I was okay with that. As she continued talking to me, my thoughts wandered to the words and tone I used earlier with my classmate. *How could I have been so nasty?* I repeated to myself. That really bothered me.

It was my first day back and all I wanted to do was complete the day without extreme special treatment. I think Mrs. Reed sensed that or thought I didn't seem ready to talk about it, which I wasn't with any type of counselor. I was still in shock and disbelief that my brother had died only three days ago. *I wonder how much she knows?* I thought, as I tried standing with my crutches and thanked her for her time. Mrs. Reed became a major catalyst for getting me all the way through high school.

Unburned Reminder

"How far that little candle throws his beams! So shines a good deed in a naughty world."
- William Shakespeare -

The following day was Thursday, March 2nd, my fifteenth birthday. Most years I woke up pretty excited, wanting to know what kind of dinner and cake Mom would make me. The friends and presents were an added bonus! I loved parties in general and people's birthdays were very important to me. I always wanted to make my friends feel as special as they should on their birthdays. I knew this year would be different and would change my life forever.

This year, I woke up thinking about what I was going to say at my brother's funeral and if I would be able to do it. I thought about what was appropriate to wear at his wake and funeral, but most of all, I woke up wondering if anybody would remember me. Would anybody feel like celebrating my life when all anybody knew and concentrated on was Chris' death? I had prepared myself for being forgotten although I desperately wanted to be acknowledged. I wasn't even sure if I wanted to celebrate either but I felt if other people weren't going to, I must not be worth celebrating.

In school, nobody had mentioned anything about my birthday to me for most of the entire day and I had started to feel quite invisible. It was towards the end of the day, when I was standing in front of my locker struggling to grab the things I needed for the next class, when an old friend of mine said, "Here, let me get that for you." Her last name began with R so her locker wasn't too far away from mine, beginning with S. She picked up the books I needed and put them in my backpack, smiled and then happily explained that she had something for me.

My friend and I had known each other since preschool and I was comforted by that fact alone. She had pulled a small, beautiful light green bag with purple tissue paper out of her locker and simply said, "Happy birthday" as she handed it over to me with a smile. I was taken aback by the gesture and looked at her in question for several seconds. *Someone had remembered me,* I thought to myself. Someone had taken the time out of their day to show their appreciation for my life. I honestly didn't care what was in the bag; she remembered *my life*, not the death of my brother. The words "thank you" could not have come any deeper from the center of my heart. I opened the gift later that day and found a beautiful white candle with the scent of magnolia. On the side of the candle, written in soft letters, were the words "brighten your life." To this day, the candle goes with me, unburned, as a reminder that I was remembered.

I don't remember anything from the rest of my birthday. I do know that it was not celebrated at home that night; I don't think that anyone, including myself, knew what to do or how to react anyway. That day, I lost a good portion of that high spirited, bubbly personality that I had identified myself with. It had really hit me hard, like a bomb exploding in my face. My brother just died and left me alone on my birthday. I became angry with him for leaving me. This was my special day and he was supposed to be there. I fell asleep on my left side where my sister Anna couldn't see my face, and I cried. I cried because it was my birthday. I cried harder for the fact that I had lost my brother and I cried hardest when I remembered that Chris was the one who would wipe my tears away when I didn't want to look like I had been crying.

Questions I'm Dying To Know

"The song has ended but the melody lingers on…"
~ Irving Berlin ~

Friday, March 3rd, I was taken out of school early to be with my family and to prepare for Chris' wake that afternoon and evening. I wasn't a part of the arrangements and had several questions running through my head as we drove into town to the funeral home. *What kind of casket did Aunt Jane and Dad pick out?*, I thought. Where were they keeping my brother and what sort of stuff had they done to his body, were some of the heavy questions that were circulating in my head. However, what I'd wondered most was, *Did Dad and Aunt Jane request an open or closed casket?* I thought if it was open, I hadn't lost the chance to see my brother one last time.

When we arrived, I realized that it was the first time our family had been all together since we got back from Maryland, including my brother Chris. One of my dad's best friends, whom we call Uncle Carl, was also with us as he had flown up from Florida to be with us. The director of the funeral home greeted us and walked us into the room we would be in for the rest of the evening. I prepared myself to see my brother lying there, very pale and stiff, in a box. I was a little surprised to find the casket closed with an 8 x 10 picture of Christopher on the top of it. It was a shiny dark wood casket about waist high with several different flower arrangements surrounding it. The smell of flowers engulfed the room, making it hard at times to just sit there with only a few others in the room.

I sat and thought about why the decision had been made to keep the casket closed. I desperately wanted to see my brother one last time, but now knowing the casket was closed, seeing him would never be a possibility for the rest of my life. I started to really think about my brother's body. Was his face that badly hurt that people would be better off not looking? Or maybe the reason why a closed casket was chosen was to save Chris' loved ones from experiencing more pain and trauma. I considered what it would be like for all my younger cousins and my little brother and sister to view his body, would it be therapeutic or more damaging? Regardless of how they might have felt, it was still my biggest regret not seeing him.

We sat there in the chairs that were so neatly set up in rows facing Chris' casket. Everyone was quiet, staring in different directions. Mom got up and walked around the room, looking at the pictures and poster boards that family and friends had made for Chris. She smelled all of the flower arrangements and returned to her seat.

Uncle Carl is much like Dad and always has a joke or a funny comment to make. My siblings and I always look forward to seeing Uncle Carl and his wife, Aunt Cindy. They refresh life with laughter. It was strange to see him here in New York and carrying a different persona with him. He was no longer joking or teasing us. He was comforting us and making sure we had everything we needed. His voice was calm and his eyes soft yet glazed with what would turn into tears. He hadn't been there more than twenty-four hours but he jumped right into looking after us. I felt safe because of that and no matter what was about to happen, I had family like Uncle Carl standing by. Now, all we had to do was wait for other people to walk in.

Line of Love

"One can pay back the loan of gold, but one dies forever in debt to those who are kind."
~ Malayan Proverb ~

Uncle Carl put Anna and one of my many cousins in charge of tissues. He told them to pass them out as people came in. He thought it would keep them busy as well as make someone possibly smirk. I watched as our family started to flow into this funeral home. I could not believe I was sitting in a funeral home, watching people arrive for my own brother. I concentrated on anything possible but the fact of why we were all here; what people were wearing, the last time I had seen them and the next time I would. I thought about what everyone had done earlier that day and how long it took them to get ready for such an occasion.

I stood at the front of the room with my family as the line to see us got longer and longer. I had to excuse myself from standing with them, as my knee was starting to bother me. It was also unbearably painful to be with my family and I couldn't stand it anymore. I sat towards the back of the room and continued to watch the line move forward, still in awe that all these people had wanted to come. There were people that came that my siblings and I had maybe met once in our lives but still came in support of our family. Some people touched my heart and brought tears to my eyes just by the way they looked at me, and others that I thought were going to be tough to see ended up not being that bad.

The first calling hours were from 3 to 5 PM and the second from 7 to 9. There were so many people waiting on the line, those who didn't get to see us during the first one had to come back to the second hours. We had so many people show up that people were turned away even at the second calling hours. I looked out the funeral home's window that faced the parking lot and looked at all the people standing on line; I couldn't see the end of it. It was at this point I realized how much we were all very loved.

I had been sitting comfortably in a large blue wing chair up against the wall. A few of both my and Chris' friends from his Boy Scout troop were sitting in a horseshoe in front of me, including Frank. Adults had come over to let us know it was okay to talk about things other than Chris and that it was okay to laugh, if we wanted to. We all looked at each other and very slowly the small circle I was sitting with had blocked out the sadness and pain around them. Everyone kept up the conversation as I just sat there listening, trying to determine whether this somewhat happy feeling I was having would be considered rude, dishonoring or inappropriate, at my brother's wake.

In between the calling hours everyone had to take a break to eat. If no one had mentioned that we had to eat I would have never realized it myself. Frank's mom came over to us and asked if I wanted to go with them for food right down the street. I was caught off guard, as I didn't expect to actually be invited places after what happened. Who would want to be around me? I smiled and accepted the offer; I was just happy that they wanted me around. It was extremely nice to leave the funeral home, take a break and be surrounded by people who loved and cared about me.

At the restaurant, it was as if nothing had happened. Everyone shared stories and talked about what was currently going on in their lives. It was a relief from the constant painful thoughts. Eating felt strange; I normally feel satisfied and fully enjoy the taste of my food but it was as if I couldn't taste the cheeseburger with fries. It looked so appetizing but my taste buds seemed to not be in the mood to work, nor was I even hungry. Oddly, I felt rejuvenated afterwards and felt I could continue with the second calling hours. I paused as we all got back into the cars and I thought, *This really is happening to me, isn't it?*

"Thank God for Your Life"

"Gratitude is the memory of the heart."
- Jean Baptiste Massieu -

The second calling hours brought more people I hadn't seen in a very long time on top of those who couldn't get in during the first hours. Again, I sat towards the back of the room looking around at all the people. Frank sat close as did several other friends. I wondered who in the room had remembered it was my birthday just yesterday and who would acknowledge it. I understood that having a young boy die tragically took precedence over another's birthday so I hadn't necessarily expected my friends or our family friends to remember; but my own family? How could *they* not know I was born just the day before, fifteen years ago?

I was angry and I felt extremely pushed aside. After I had accepted that this would just be the way it is and my life would fade into the chaos, someone gave me hope, the acknowledgement that I so badly wanted. My aunt quietly came over to me with tears rolling down her face and kneeled down by my chair. She took out a beautiful light blue envelope with my name on it, gave it to me, and whispered in my ear saying, "I never forgot about you and I never will."

She stood up and expressed her understanding towards my confusion on whether to celebrate or not and told me it was okay to open the card whenever I wanted, whether that day or a year after. My eyes started to haze over with water as I opened the card and read the note inside. It read, "So you decided to open this card. I am proud of you! I know this is an extremely painful time and people might not remember you while they concentrate on the tragedy that happened to your family, but if I know you and your strength, you'll continue to touch lives just by being you. Today I celebrate you being alive and thank God for your life." There were other people that really touched my heart at the wake, but nobody else acknowledged my life the way my aunt did.

A friend I had known since I was real little approach me, balling her eyes out, repeating how sorry she was and explaining she didn't know what else to say. I was instantly brought back to the times I played with her and my brother Chris had decided to join in. Sometimes he was a true brother and teased us until we couldn't stand it anymore, and other times he peacefully joined us in whatever we decided to do. In fact, everyone I saw at the wake brought back at least one memory I had of my brother. Some made me want to laugh out loud and others actually hurt my chest, being so painful to think about.

As I sat there in the back of the room, my Uncle John and Aunt Jean came over to me with my two cousins. The fun we all had together was only comparable to being beyond a rainbow. The creativity, laughter, and adventure we shared with them, is something I've never experienced with anyone else in my life. Their faces registered in my memory instantaneously and my eyes began to tear. I couldn't understand why this moment was so painful for me, more so than with any other person. There are just some people in your life that have taught you so much about life, who take you to another world whenever you're with them, that in moments like these, all you can do is allow yourself to feel everything, knowing you are surrounded by comfort. I felt protected with the four of them by my side and I was afraid of what I'd feel the moment they'd leave.

Every memory I ever had of my brother came flooding to the front of my mind and replayed itself just as if it were happening right there for the first time. I was overwhelmed with intense pain even when thinking of happy memories. It is at these times in our lives we all wish pain could be erased from our repertoire of emotions, or do we?

The Sweet Taste of Sleep

"I cannot stand being awake, the pain is too much."
~ Unknown Author ~

That evening, March 3rd, my mom did the best she could to do something for my birthday. A little cake from Carvel was bought because Mom was in no state of mind to spend the time making one. We ate cake as happily as we could and spent some time with my dad's brother and his wife.

When I was younger, we didn't see my uncle too often. Despite this, they knew it was my birthday and brought a gift; the gesture had warmed my heart. If it were possible to have your heart smile, mine did, although it didn't quite make it to my face. I'm not sure it was possible to outwardly smile during those days, those hours and moments. I remember exactly where we were all sitting when I received the gift and the exact way I opened the white box. They had gotten me a beautiful light blue flowered skirt with a matching light blue top. What people remember after experiencing a traumatic event intrigues me. What caused me to remember the detail of my present and not some of the major conversations or events, I will never know. I still have the outfit and wear it often, at times remembering how and where I got it.

I opened the gift rather late, as the calling hours did not end until 9 PM. By the time we arrived back home, had a snack and cake, I didn't open the present until around 10:30 PM. Chris' funeral was the next day and I could tell my parents and grandparents were very tired; emotionally and physically drained from the day. We all appreciated the people that spent time with us afterwards but sleep sounded like hot chocolate after coming in from the cold, wet snow; simply amazing. All I wanted to do was curl up, let my eyelids slowly cover my eyes and fall into a dream. Any dream would have been better than what my reality had become. If I were lucky, I'd fall asleep and never have to leave the dream world my mind would create. When I dream, it's fairly detailed and usually pretty happy; I desperately wanted and needed that.

I was exhausted and it felt good to just do nothing. After our house became silent I lay in bed thinking about what I was going to say at my brother's funeral the following day, and whether or not I would be able to actually do it in front of everyone. I had prepared a few things to say on paper, hoping it would be halfway good enough to read for others. Although I wanted rest terribly, my mind would never get the rest it needed anytime soon.

Finding Comfort in a Butterfly

"I've learned that goodbye's will always hurt, pictures will never replace having been there, memories good and bad will bring tears, and words can never replace feelings."
~ Unknown Author ~

I woke up dreading the day, March 4th. Today would be the last day I had that the world would allow me to really say goodbye to my brother. I opened my closet door to search for something, anything that seemed nice enough to wear to a sibling's funeral. I looked at my blue sweaters and what little black clothing I had. Generally, I always saw people wear black to funerals and to wakes of loved ones. Black was just not my brother; he wasn't plain or ordinary. In fact, he was quite the opposite, very vibrant and looking for new adventure or mischief.

I finally chose a long grey skirt that came to my ankles and a red t-shirt with a silver butterfly on it. Some say butterflies symbolize life after death and that love is eternal. I chose to wear the butterfly to ease my pain, reminding myself that Chris was free, although somewhere inside me I did not want him to be. I wanted him here, I wanted to hear his voice and see the dimples on his face.

My entire family met at our church just fifteen minutes away. Mom and Dad's insurance company covered them to have a rent-a-car to be able to travel and figure everything out. I don't know how I felt about being in a rent-a-car; it prompted me to think about the fact that we didn't have a vehicle anymore; it had been totaled.

Every family member from my immediate family to cousins of cousins and further distant family were at the church. It was so nice to have all of my family in one place but so terrible that it had to be for something so tragic. We had family come from all over the country, from New York to Colorado and Arizona down to Florida and the Carolinas. Again, every person I saw brought back at least one memory of my brother. Some people were really hard to make eye contact with at the funeral; one in particular was my Uncle Brian.

My uncle always played with Chris and me I when we were little, without complaint. He loved playing any sort of games with my brother and became that cool, "older brother" that Chris and I would never have. Some of my favorite memories with Uncle Brian were having water fights with super soakers in our backyard or playing "man hunt," a flashlight tag game, in the dark with him and Uncle Rich. Only months before our accident Chris mentioned he wanted to play football, but Mom thought it was too dangerous, so he told Uncle Brian, who had played when he was younger. Uncle Brian nonchalantly told Chris he would talk Mom into letting him play and he did. Chris was so excited that he would be playing the following season! It was difficult and very painful to watch Uncle Brian hold back the tears as we gathered before the funeral, knowing Chris would never play football or any other game with him ever again. It is extremely hard to watch those whom you admire and look up to in some of the worst pain you'll probably ever see them in; I just hated to see my family like this.

Everyone was there and we were now waiting for others to be seated. We couldn't see the sanctuary from the room we were in so I had no idea who was there. Our pastor clarified how the service would go and asked if we had any questions. I asked when I would be speaking and if I could bring my little cousin Alivia up with me. She was only six years old, so my aunt had helped her write down some things she wanted to say. Everything was set, everyone was seated, and all we needed to do was walk towards saying goodbye. This would be one of the hardest walks of my life.

Trumpeting of Emotions

"Never shall I forget the time I spent with you."
~ Ludwig Van Beethoven ~

As we walked towards the sanctuary, I saw the social hall beneath it, filled with people who couldn't fit upstairs in the 250-person capacity sanctuary that was already overflowing. There were TVs set up for those in the social hall to be able to view the funeral and people were flowing out of that room as well. I never imagined so many people would come. I saw faces of those I only met once, those that only knew me as a baby and those who saw me every day. I continued walking up the stairs towards the sanctuary and could hear the sound of trumpets getting louder.

When we entered the sanctuary, I saw a friend of Chris' from the church and his father playing a trumpet duet to "For All the Saints" played at some Christian funerals. Music has always played a very special part in my life. Certain songs and notes put together have some magic to them and will touch your inner soul if you let it. Music has the ability to doubly intensify what I already feel. I told myself I would try my hardest not to cry, to be strong for my family. Why is it that we feel it necessary to not cry during an occasion that perfectly calls for it? Maybe it's because we've labeled it as a sign of weakness, that it would mean we couldn't handle certain situations. Has anyone ever thought about what the world would be like if crying was thought to be a sign of love for what you've lost and there was no shame in it? The music I was hearing had caused my "strong" stature and heart to begin to break down and I was finding it difficult to fight back my tears.

I began to scan the church and briefly saw those sitting towards the back. Among them were Chris' principal and vice principal, some of his teachers, and various extended family members. Their faces, as they turned around to watch us walk in, sunk my heart. I had never seen more sad faces in one place and certainly not on the account of my family or me. In front of us was Chris' Boy Scout troop in their uniforms and lined up in pairs. There were about six pairs and so I couldn't see that my brother was behind them in a casket being carried by other Boy Scouts he had been closer with, such as Frank and his dad, who was one of the scout leaders. They all began to march in, up the center aisle; my immediate family and my grandparents followed after his casket. *My brother is in there*, I kept thinking. I wanted so desperately to open it and get him out, to hold him. Maybe if I held him close enough, squeezed him, he'd come back.

We sat in the front right pew, closest to the pulpit. I was sitting at my brother's funeral, my brother who was only twelve years old. Although it was never my responsibility to completely protect my brother, I sat there thinking I should have done something to save his life, anything. Staring at his casket, my grave thoughts were interrupted by our pastor who began the service by welcoming everyone. He then welcomed some of the Boy Scouts to come forward and speak.

In the area I grew up, it is a big deal to be a Boy Scout and a great honor to become an Eagle Scout, hence the reason why he was escorted in by his troop. They shared stories and expressed how much Chris would be missed. Frank had planned on being one of those who spoke and stood up there with the other scouts, but I could see the pain on his face was too great. He stepped away and gave someone else the floor to speak. It wasn't obvious to the room that he told someone else to speak, but I saw it. It tortured me to see him that way, in such pain. I felt the urge to go up there and save him, to protect him like he had always done for me.

Some of the stories the scouts shared made me laugh, but most were what we call bittersweet. It is such a shame that stories so great are only told at the person's funeral or afterwards. I wonder if any of those who have passed on were ever told before of how much they meant to others or what their life brought to the world. Every life changes and affects the world more than we give credit.

Some of Chris' friends from church spoke after the scouts and again shared poems and memories about his life. These few boys had mentioned what a patient, older brother he was as they watched him allow his little brother, Matthew, to tag along with him almost everywhere. This caused them to remember not to take their siblings for granted when and if they ever decide to "follow" them around.

One of Chris' closest friends from school was the last of his friends to speak. This boy spent numerous hours with my brother, shared his inner most secrets with him, and, of course, did all the normal, trouble-making "boy" activities with him. He spoke about my brother's love for food and the way he had always made him laugh. Chris was definitely known for his humor and perpetual smile, as other speakers mentioned. It took such bravery for his friend to get up there and I couldn't believe we were all having to do this for my twelve-year-old brother. Most everyone who had spoken also commented on how his life was cut so short, how sad and tragic it was that he didn't get to live a full life. It would be my turn next. My heart was racing.

Walking Towards Goodbye

"We must embrace pain and burn it as fuel for our journey."
~ Kenji Miyazawa ~

Speaking at my brother's funeral was no easy task but I am certainly grateful that I had the strength and courage to do so. I hobbled up the three stairs to the altar with prepared speeches in one hand and my cousin Alivia's hand in the other. As I read what Alivia and her mom had written, I felt my emotions rising as I was immediately taken back to the memories she had chosen to share.

Chris used to play all sorts of games with our cousins and without fail would get Alivia to laugh so hard she could barely breathe. Because of this and the numerous silly expressions and statements he made, she nicknamed him "crazy Christopher." My cousin was young, just like Matthew, only six years old. I had no idea how to comfort her or how much she understood, but I tried the best I could by lightly rubbing her back and putting my arm around her. I finished relaying her message and took a deep breath before beginning mine. Alivia never knew that just her presence next to me was comforting, kept me calm and ultimately saved me from falling apart as I read what I had prepared. It truly is amazing what a child's presence can do.

I honestly couldn't tell you that I remember what words I used or even how I said what I did. What I do remember from my speech was the message I tried to convey; my brother was over all good-hearted and always went out of his way for other people. The story I shared was about his last week alive. With the money my siblings and I are each given on vacation, he spent it all buying small gifts for his friends. My parents kept asking, "Chris, don't you want to buy yourself something?" He replied with a satisfied "No." His choice to buy for everyone else was incredibly humbling for me, as his older sister, watching a twelve-year-old boy give everything. I finished my speech heavy-hearted and slowly made my way back down to the front pew with my cousin.

So many people wanted to be involved in his funeral and they were. People I had never met in my life played music or sang. The songs that were sung or played really tugged at my heart. How could music affect me so much? I didn't want it to, not in front of all those people. Music reaches into the inner depths of my heart where no words or feelings could possibly touch. The songs chosen for his funeral are still painful to hear as they each bring me right back to that front right pew of my brother's funeral.

What got me analyzing this tragic event the most were the words of our pastor as he sent everyone home with a light, but very profound message. He had heard several people mention how terrible it is that a twelve-year-old-boy lost his life and would never get to experience "this" or "that." "While this is true," he had stated, "It does not mean his life was any less *full* than anyone's here today." He was right; my brother's life was very full. He was loved by so many and was fortunate to be part of a large, loving family. He had friends just like everyone else; he had crushes just like every other boy and he experienced so much in his twelve years. This message reminded me to not always look at what I would never have with him but to be thankful for what my brother had already given me. While this is true, it is incredibly easier to say you'll think this way than actually doing it, especially when the pain is so great.

The time had really come, the time to say "goodbye." Our pastor said a prayer and my brother was again escorted down the aisle, this time to *Amazing Grace.* I knew this was it, the last point in time that the rest of the world would allow me to really grieve. I felt the world expected me to pour every bit of my pain, frustration, anger, and hurt all into his casket and bury it with him; as if covering it up deep under dirt would make it all go away.

Although his funeral was a painful experience, I desperately did not want to leave, in fear of knowing these would be my last goodbyes. As I followed my brother down the aisle, this time I could see people's faces, all with tears running down their cheeks. I felt the music, the trumpets and organ, I heard the powerful words, "Amazing grace, how sweet the sound," and I saw the hurting faces. I was not ready to let go and I lost it. I sobbed uncontrollably down the aisle with crutches, barely able to hold myself up, and walked out of the church. That was the *worst* and most traumatic walk of my life.

A Shovelful of Love

"Truly wonderful the mind of a child is."
Yoda: Star Wars Trilogy

Standing outside, having fresh air and few people around was relieving. Although it was the beginning of March, I don't remember it being cold. I had no jacket on and the sun was shining bright. Family, friends, acquaintances and people I had never met began to pour out of the church. Several friends from church and others I knew from the town, Pleasantville, soon surrounded me. Each one gave me their condolences and a hug. Some asked how I ever got up in front of so many people during a time like this. They continued with saying how strong and brave I was. Little did they know I had begun to fall apart from the inside out.

The little town was packed with people concentrated all in one area; there was no way people were getting out without assistance. Police cars were stationed in various areas to control the traffic flowing out of several parking lots. Pleasantville town police and one small fire truck had even escorted my brother in his hearse to the border of our hometown. Our town police were waiting at the border, as they would be the ones to escort my brother to his final resting place. Chris had always wanted to be a fireman so our family found it fitting that he was escorted by those who currently served the people of New York. *Who thought to do all this?* I wondered. Who thought to have escorts and police watching the traffic or even to put TV's in other rooms of the church? I certainly wouldn't have thought of any of that myself, although I was only fifteen. Someone had expected a very large crowd and had been prepared for everything.

The long line of cars paraded into the cemetery and arrived at the section Chris would be buried in. He had one of the most beautiful spots, on top of a hill, under a tree over-looking a small mountain range. Everyone had gathered around as last words were said. I paid close attention to the expressions on others' faces, intrigued by their emotions.

Matthew had been a brave little soldier this entire time and told Dad that he wanted to help bury Christopher. I kept reminding myself that this little boy was only five years old, coping and grasping with the fact that his older brother was being put into the ground. This moment took me back to Matt's hospital room when he found out Chris was not coming home with us. Matt's strength was incredible and again I saw the same stature, the same bravery on his face just as he had shown in the hospital. Never underestimate what a child can endure, and the strength and wisdom that they will acquire from it. And, at the same time, remember that endurance does not mean it won't be hard or they don't need comfort.

Someone had brought Matt's colored toy shovel and Dad helped him scoop the first shovelful of dirt on top of his casket. He did it with such pride and love. I lost control of my emotions again and the tears streamed down my cheeks like rain. I didn't care if everyone had been looking at me, I just could not stop staring at the casket with that one small pile of dirt on it.

The Show Must Go On

"Change is never easy, you fight to hold on, and you fight to let go."
~ *The Wonder Years* ~

The last thing I can remember from the week my brother died was the meal after the burial. I'd like to know who started that tradition of having a large meal that anyone could attend. Nobody knows how to act because the gathering is not a happy occasion and I felt strange having a "good" time eating with everyone. It was held at our local Elks Club, a place for public events, and those who mostly came, other than family, were from or really close to our town.

It is one of our family traditions to put on a play whenever the cousins get together. It has been since we started performing *The Wizard of Oz* in my Aunt Jane's backyard. Acting, dancing and performing has always been one of my favorite things to do and as the oldest cousin I took it upon myself to direct the plays. Our plays became such a tradition that we began putting on performances at every special occasion, whether it was someone's favorite show/play or a performance about their life. Chris would always play a vital role in every show we put on because he was the only older boy cousin we had on the east coast. We have a cousin who lives out in Arizona although we only see him during family reunions. He and Chris would pal around together when we did see him, as they were the two boys closest in age. Oh how my cousin loved his time spent with Chris.

My sister and other cousins had decided during this reception that they wanted to put on a play of Chris' life. They asked me if I would help direct it. It felt like several minutes before I could give them an answer. I declined the offer politely. I didn't feel up to performing or even creating a performance. I knew my cousins and sister would do just as well without me and so told them, "I have a few people to talk to but you guys should still do it."

It was really different getting to watch rather than be a part of it. I sat there as they went through memories they had chosen to recreate. Like the time Chris and our cousin went boogie boarding down at Myrtle Beach and we couldn't get them out of the water, or the time we went to an amusement park out in Pennsylvania, getting our other cousin to go on whatever crazy rides we were in line for. I thought about how these memories of him would fade over time in everyone's lives. *Is this how my brother would remain alive, by telling stories and family traditions such as this?* I wondered.

Leaving this meal would mean the end of the day; the end of the day meant the end of saying goodbye to my brother. I wasn't too sure if I wanted this day to end or not. But the inevitable would not care what I, Michelle, wanted. These are of the last detailed, daily memories I have after the death of my brother. Although painful, I hold the memories with a vice grip close to my heart.

"Human Pain does not let go of its grip at one point in time. Rather, it works its way out of our consciousness over time. There is a season of sadness. A season of anger. A season of tranquility. A season of hope."
- Robert Veninga -

Numb

"Numbing the pain for awhile will make it worse when you finally feel it."
- J.K. Rowling -

Maybe you have experienced something similar to what I have and you just cannot get it through your head that someone you love is no longer with you, or you have experienced such a loss that leaves you lying on the bottom of the Grand Canyon, helpless. For a lack of a better phrase, it truly and utterly sucks. I had hit rock bottom and would begin living the darkest time of my life. Although it had seemed as if I fared the news well and continued on living my life outwardly, I was within the deepest of oceans and the darkest of forests inside my soul. My heart felt like a black hole with one grain of sand representing light. That one grain became the only hope I had, knowing I hadn't lost it all and maybe, some day, I'd have more light.

Following the week of our accident and Chris' funeral I had continued to go to school, refusing to take a day off even if I knew I should have. I kept telling myself, *You are just fine, you can do this.* I went through the everyday motions, becoming number to the world with each day that passed. I found myself missing huge chunks of my life. Being so numb took the pain away but it also meant feeling like I didn't exist in those moments. I became so numb, my brain began to repress what had happened and I regressed in time to thinking that I had not lost my brother. It could've possibly been the fact that I didn't want to admit my brother was no longer with me the way I would remember or that the pain was so great that my body had to resort to last measures in order to give itself a break.

Either way, repressing it only made the hurt more excruciatingly painful when something, anything, triggered the fact that my brother was, in fact, gone.

A few weeks afterwards, I had awakened to my daily alarm clock, preparing for the school day. Normally, after I woke up and got dressed, I went downstairs to wake Chris up. This particular morning, I stumbled, half asleep, into Matt's room where he was sound asleep. I tried to wake Chris up on the top bunk bed when I had finally realized I was reaching at bunched up covers and several stuffed animals he had acquired over his twelve years of life. The emotions I felt the second I was brought back to reality can only equate to someone reaching into my chest and squeezing my heart, trying to stop it from beating. I froze and remembered why being numb felt so comforting. I didn't have much time to wallow in the emotions; Frank would be at my door in just ten minutes.

There had been hundreds of people surrounding my family and me for weeks after Chris died. Everyone was extremely noticeable the week of his death and just about three weeks following. The people began to fade as "enough time" had surely passed to where none of us needed the comfort or presence of people. It always seems to be that people make themselves known during the immediacy of a death or a tragedy, when the person has not even had enough time to grasp the fact that they experienced a loss and life would forever change thence forth. When the loss decides to hit you smack in the face and then makes its way to your heart, you look around for all those people and it gets lonelier and lonelier as few have stayed longer than a few weeks to a couple of months.

Almost every single person I came in contact with the week Chris passed away had in some form offered their ear to listen or their hands to help with anything I ever needed. I was grateful to everyone and knew they truly meant it, but it wasn't so much during this time that I needed the offers, it was when the world seemed to fade and I wondered where everyone had gone that I needed the presence of other people's "light." To what extent are the offers good for? How long do they last and what would be an appropriate time frame to ask for help? I wasn't comfortable enough with the answers I gave myself to those questions and so never really knew how to ask for help. And no matter how much help I would receive, I always seemed alone. It is without a doubt true what people say, that when one person is missing, the whole world seems depopulated.

Tolerance for Insensitivity

"It's what you do, unthinking, that makes the quick tear start; the tear may be forgotten – but the hurt stays in the heart."
~ Ella Higginson ~

If it isn't bad enough that you have to lose someone you love, on top of that there are just some extremely insensitive people that somehow cross your path, making it so much worse. Why? It always seems those are the people that come around when you want or need them the least. Sometimes the most hurtful and dumbest statements come from those who are closest to you, making it harder to understand why it was said.

Within weeks of Chris' funeral, I was walking the halls of my high school with a close friend. It was fifth period and we didn't have the same class together but our classrooms happened to be directly across from each other. As we walked through the language hallway, she caught me off guard when she asked, "How come you're not sad or seem to care that your brother died?" I don't remember the conversation we were having beforehand, whether a question like that flowed with it or was completely random. Either way, how do you reply to such a question without bursting into tears, becoming full of rage or simply just walking away from the person with no warning?

It was rather difficult for me to stand there with her and calmly reply; somehow I managed. "I don't think I understand," I said in a questioning voice. She repeated her question with clarification, "Well, it just doesn't seem like you're that upset about it. You don't cry or tell me you are hurting." My anger began to rise as I responded with a slightly elevated voice. "So, because I don't cry in front of *you* and I don't share with *you* that I hurt, implies the fact that I don't seem to care that my brother died?" The conversation lasted only seconds more as we were both irritated with each other's comments. I was baffled that anyone would say such a thing, let alone a friend who said she cared.

I am sure if you have lost a loved one that there was some sort of comment made that was completely unnecessary or puzzling as to why it was said. "Things are getting back to normal now?" "He's in a better place, take comfort in that" or "He wouldn't want you to be sad or to cry." These are just some of the various comments that were heard along the way, especially immediately following Chris' passing. He's in a better place? Well, of course, he is, but he was perfectly happy here with us, thank you very much. People do have the best intentions, most of the time, and there is no possible way to know what does and what does not offend each and every person as they grieve. I believe that no matter what is said to the person, it builds and strengthens them into a new, wiser person. Although it is hurtful and never a pleasant experience to hear such comments, then or ever, it has made me who I am today.

As a teen, I found that it was more difficult to hear such comments because they came from everyone: adults, peers, others a bit older and those slightly younger. I was already in transition between being a child and becoming an adult, which made it more difficult to figure out from whom I could find the most comfort. I found great comfort from the children in my life; so simple, pure and truly understanding of the pain. Maybe they didn't know or comprehend the words but they felt it and they saw it. Although there were several who made unnecessary comments, there were just as many, if not more, who would make a considerable difference in my life.

The Gift of Anonymity

"Giving is most blessed and most acceptable
when the donor remains completely anonymous."
~ Moses Maimonides ~

I was stubborn to my own emotions, not allowing myself to feel even the slightest bit of pain, but who does actually want to feel the pain? I was determined not to allow such a traumatic loss to control my life. In fact, I tried very hard to do so. Unbeknownst to me, in trying so hard not to have it control my life, I had given the pain and the loss full control. By not allowing myself to hurt, I had dug myself an even deeper hole in which only I had the power to help myself get out, by climbing one hand at a time.

I continued on doing as many events as I could fit in my schedule, leaving no time for pain to leak in. Part of why I never allowed myself to hurt was because I was angry. I was angry at the world for people's bad decisions and hurtful comments, at God for allowing this to happen and for putting me through such agonizing pain and, finally, I was angry with my brother for leaving. How could he leave me?

Although I had begun to dig myself a hole, there were friends and people I never knew that insisted on helping, on making my life as easy as possible and, quite frankly, more fun. I would have never asked for help or for the things that friends had done. I am forever grateful for their insistence and wanting something better for my life. It was towards the end of March that year that two boys from my youth group and several good friends decided to give me a birthday party during the time our youth group met. I was completely flattered to even be remembered and it truly meant the world to me.

I spoke with one of the two boys almost every day after school and into the summer. There was something about his voice and his sensitive personality that automatically comforted me no matter what our conversations were about. We confided in each other on several occasions and nobody would know that we had spoken so frequently and freely to each other. We liked it that way. Although our close friendship was within a brief time period, I will always remember him as a safe haven for my thoughts and feelings.

Not only were friends very much a part of my grief, random people that we met maybe once, or complete strangers, contributed to my family's life and grieving process during those months following the accident. People were doing the simplest of things for us to try to make the loss as "easy" as possible. I could never write down the amount of stuff that people did for our family as that could be a novel in and of itself but there are two prominent memories I have that at times bring me to tears.

There had been a long list of people who had signed up to bring us food, enough to last us several months, well into the summer. Some of those who signed up we knew well, others less so, but they still wanted to bring us a hot meal. It touched my heart that so many wanted to do something so simple for us, bring dinner. Every night we had someone different over who would spend a few minutes with us asking about all sorts of things. It had been incredibly nice to see someone different every day without the chaos of a funeral. In fact, my brain absorbed the memory better of those who spent the time to bring us dinner more so than the hundreds of people who attended the funeral. And why wouldn't it? I was soaked with adrenaline and shock with so many people around.

The other memory was a tremendous gift that if not given would have put our family in much worse of a position. A third party had called to inform us that there was someone who wanted to help get us a new car/van but wished to remain anonymous. The third party gave the impression that the car would be bought and our family could repay in our own time. This extremely generous gesture had brought us a new vehicle, as we no longer had one. Dad had just donated his second car right before we left for our Florida trip with the idea of buying a new one when we returned. Having an accident left us with no transportation other than the rented one from the insurance company.

It would have been extremely hard for my family to be able to buy two cars at once and, quite frankly, we barely would have been able to afford one with all the other expenses we had incurred due to the unexpected death. My parents were asked to go down to the dealer and pick out the van they wanted. After choosing, they were told everything was taken care of and that our family would never have to pay a cent at any point. The car was to be a gift to our family.

There are no words to describe how amazing a gift this was for my family. With the help of an anonymous donor we had a brand new van and my parents could not have been more grateful. Who would give us such a generous gift? It puzzled me for such a long time. I so desperately wanted to know who it was, to be able to thank them whole-heartedly. To this day, we still do not know who gave us the beautiful vehicle. Although for years I had walked around in life wondering if I had ever come in contact with the donor or saw them frequently, I have come to realize how truly great of a gift they gave us; the gift of anonymity. I cannot speak for my family but I know if ever I knew who graciously gave it to us, I would feel the need to pay them back, and that was not their purpose. Maybe someday, whoever bought the van will reveal themselves; until then I wish for the person or people to know how much their generosity meant to us.

If only they truly knew.

Remembering Chip

"If there ever comes a day when we can't be together, keep me in your heart, I'll stay there forever."
~ Winnie the Pooh ~

Spring brought new life and fresh air. It was amazing to see the green grass and the beautiful little crocuses and daffodils that grew all around our yard. Just knowing that other things were alive and continuously growing seemed to lighten the idea of death, if only slightly. I came home from school one afternoon to find my parents crying in Chris and Matt's room as they cleaned out all of Chris' clothes and stuff that would not be needed anymore. They asked me what to do with the gifts Chris bought over this past vacation for his friends; they had no idea what was intended for each.

I took it upon myself to figure out whom each gift belonged to. As I searched for the names Chris had shared with me the night he bought everything at Disney, I realized that I had a connection with each person in some way. Coincidence? I don't know. What I do know is that the gifts he bought had such deep meaning for those who received them. I hadn't put much thought into the meaning of the words my brother used as he described to me why he was buying certain gifts for these individuals until I was left alone to figure out what gift belonged to what girl.

"So why are you getting this?" I remember asking Chris as he took this beautiful white polar bear with a cub, made out of solid sand up to the cash register. He smirked at me like a younger brother would when they want to say something like, "And you want to know, *why?*" He put up no resistance and told me that this particular girl absolutely loved polar bears and they held special meaning to her. He continued by saying, "I want her to know I listen." I was quite impressed and told him it was a very nice thing to do.

The second gift I remember, as he described the meaning, caught my ear a bit more, although I never in a million years would have put anything together. He found a cute Chip (as in Chip and Dale) stuffed animal for another friend of his. Without asking this time, he told me he was getting this for a friend who often told him he has the cutest dimples and that he reminded her of a chipmunk. Chris paused and then nonchalantly said, "It's so that she will always remember me for the name she gave me, Dimples."

I couldn't help but wonder if Chris knew something was going to happen. Could he have known he wouldn't be returning to our hometown with us? No, not possible is it? Whether he did or did not know, the comments he made were clear that he wanted these girls to know how he felt. Chris had gifts for others but these were the two that really stood out in my memory. I knew who to give the delicate polar bears to as Chris had mentioned her name. I arranged for a time to meet with her during school hours because I had no other way of getting in contact with her. I walked over to the middle school, next to our high school, with a bittersweet excitement in knowing this girl would finally get the gift my brother intended her to have.

I could see the uneasiness on her face and could only imagine what thoughts were running through her head. We had never met before but there we were, face to face, knowing full well why we were brought together. I gave her the gift and told her why my brother wanted her to have it; for her to know he listened. She didn't have to say anything to me, her tears and choked up expression said it all. I was instantly taken back to the way I felt when Aunt Jane brought back the snow globe that Chris found for me. I knew it hurt terribly that Chris was not the one bringing this gift back for her, but I also knew that the gift would be what she remembered him by for as long as she kept it.

It took me much longer, years in fact, to find the girl who called Chris "Dimples." When I learned of who it was, I was surprised to find that I had already known and established a relationship with her after Chris died. I felt relieved to know it had been her all along but surprised that I hadn't figured it out sooner. Until every rightful owner had her gift, I didn't feel at peace. Somehow it all turned out just the way it should have and I was happy to finally see "unfinished business" finished. They were all so grateful to receive them, whenever that time had come. It is extremely difficult to receive a gift that you know came from someone you loved and cared about but has passed away. You grasp tightly to that only tangible thing you are left with, in hopes of never letting go.

One Last Ride

"The greater your capacity to love, the greater your capacity to feel the pain."
~ Jennifer Aniston ~

One night, a couple of months after the accident, I brushed my teeth, put my pajamas on and got in bed as I usually did. I rolled over into my favorite cozy spot, closed my eyes and fell asleep. I soon found myself within a dream as real as what we deem real. It almost felt like I hadn't fallen asleep because I was now tossing and turning in my bed, trying to get comfortable when a bright light appeared at the end of my bedpost. The light was so bright I couldn't see anything but that. When it was gone, there at the end of my bed, stood my brother, smiling.

I was completely startled and immediately sat up, backing as far as I could up against my headboard. *Is this real or am I dreaming?* I said to myself. He walked slowly over to the side of my bed and gently said, "Do not be afraid, it's really me." I stared at him and blinked as if it were possible I was hallucinating. He asked me to touch his hands in proof that he was really there, standing in front of me. I reached out slowly, with a little hesitation and finally touched his hand. I couldn't believe what I was feeling and immediately moved both my hands to his. He felt as real as I am, as if I were to take one hand and touch my other one. I knew deep down inside that Chris was dead and so I couldn't understand how this was possible, to feel not just his presence but also his flesh.

Chris began speaking again, "Hold my hand tight, I want to take you somewhere," he said. I didn't quite understand what he was trying to do and he sensed that. "Trust me," he continued. I squeezed his hand and soon found myself somewhere other than my own bed. I looked around and quickly realized we were in Sea World. The park was completely empty and we were standing in front of the ride we had gone on several times only months prior. Whatever this was, it sure seemed like my very own heaven. Chris seemed so excited and began running ten feet in front of me towards the ride. He stopped and turned around, realizing I hadn't followed him. I was still taking in the fact that we were even in the park. *How did we get here so fast*, I thought. My thoughts were promptly pushed aside when Chris said, "Are ya coming? Let's go, there's no line!"

Chris and I kept going on and off the ride, each time making different faces at the camera. I was beside myself with excitement and soon forgot about how or why I was there. I was with my brother, in a theme park and that was all that mattered to me in that moment. I had no worries in the world and I felt no pain; wherever we were I never wanted to leave.

We had just gotten off the ride for the umpteenth time and without thought I began to run back on when I turned around to realize that my brother hadn't followed me this time. I asked him, just like he had asked me, if he was coming. He kept standing there, gave me a bittersweet smile and sighed with his head slightly tilted to the right side. I knew by this look that he wasn't coming, so I walked back over to him and asked why he didn't want to come. "I can't," he said. "It's time for me to go. "I came to finish some things and it's time to go."

I was utterly confused as to why he brought me here. I hadn't even gotten the chance to ask him anything and now he was leaving? "Well, can I come with you?" I asked. "No," he simply replied. "You can't come where I'm going. You have to stay here." "But why?" I said with painful frustration; I was here with him now, what made it so that I couldn't continue to be with him? "Someone needs you. You're going to help them," my brother said to me. I couldn't think of anything else to say, being so confused, so I kept listening to his words. "I gotta go now but I love you and I'll always be with you." As I was mustering up a meek "I love you" with tears, the same bright light came and I could no longer see my brother.

I blinked and found myself back in my own bed. I sat up, remembering everything that had just happened and began a new day. Whatever happened that night put me more at peace, knowing my brother was okay. I somehow felt more connected with Chris and wished for more experiences like the one I just had because this seemed to be all I had left of my brother. It was one thing to be left with pictures and memories but to be left with real to life dreams where I could actually feel him, was closer to seeming like Chris never left. I didn't want to lose that.

Fighting for Another Love

"Solitude is a good place to visit but a poor place to stay."
- Josh Billings -

When I look back on that time of my life, with each day that passed I had become more and more depressed, although at the time I didn't know that's what was happening. I spent most of my free time alone either listening to music or watching movies I hadn't seen in awhile; I remember enjoying that time to myself. It wasn't that I didn't enjoy the time with others, I just really enjoyed the time alone. It's hard to determine whether my enjoyment for solitude was due to such a traumatic loss, to just being a normal teenager learning and trying to individualize myself, or quite possibly both.

Although I spent more and more time alone, during the rest of my freshmen school year I had clung to being able to leave the house and dance. Dancing has always been one of my favorite hobbies and remains so. It tortured me not to be able to dance for a few months while I let my knee heal. But just because I had an injured knee, I didn't let it stop me from attending the classes to watch the new combinations.

I sat on the side memorizing each move and absorbing whatever "high" I could get from dance. Since I was very little, my legs, head, and heart have been beating to the rhythm of music. This passion of mine would lead to the release of an intense amount of emotion that I could never set free any other way. Each grieving "tool" I have used over the years serves its own purpose. What I could express with music could never be what I express with dancing, and vice versa.

Because my knee was so badly injured, doctors told me I would not and could not dance for quite some time. *Quite some time? Well what does that mean?* I thought. *Does that mean a month, two months, a year, what?* The orthopedic doctor gave me roughly six months to recuperate. I was crushed and, honestly, quite angry that another "love" in my life would be taken away from me. "Well, at least this is something you can go back to," people told me; as opposed to never being able to get my brother back. My stubbornness had certainly kicked in and I was absolutely determined to get back on my own two feet, dancing and ready to perform by the end of May.

I practiced in my head for weeks and stretched on my own in my room, still spending more and more time alone. I finally went into dance class about a month before the performance, prepared to join the others. My teacher wasn't too sure if I should have been working so hard so early but saw my determination and allowed me to continue. "If you feel like you cannot do something, even the slightest thing, sit out," she told me, with doubt in her voice that she was even allowing me to do so. I undoubtedly was sore afterwards but it felt great!

I was able to perform that May and smiled throughout the entire performance. I had been so proud of myself until I realized afterwards that I only had three family members in the audience instead of four. My sister, Anna, was in the same dance recital so it was usually my parents and two brothers watching. At the end of the performance, our parents usually had flowers waiting; Chris and Matt would give them to us. That year, May of 2000, we did not receive flowers, for whatever reason. It was again one of those moments where I had been reminded of what I had lost. It is extremely challenging to think of the good times I was given with my brother when pain like this seems to take over, following me around like a black cloud above my head.

Play-Doh Is Lots of Fun

*"Adolescence represents an inner emotional upheaval,
a struggle between the eternal human wish to cling to the past and the
equally powerful wish to get on with the future."*
~ Louise J. Kaplan ~

Before summer had come, sometime in May, my parents had decided they wanted us to all see a counselor, as a family. I couldn't believe it, what were they thinking? Chris had only been gone just under three months. I was not at all ready to be talking to some stranger, let alone in front of my entire family. I was quite irritated that they thought we were *all* ready for therapy or counseling.

After school one day, my parents took us to see someone. I don't know what her credentials were or even what organization or agency she was with, we were just seeing "someone." The place had many offices and color covered the walls and items that were in the waiting area. We were called into a fairly large room that had several toys including wooden trains, Slinkies, and a red car with the yellow top that most kids remember from their childhood. My sister and brother quickly made themselves comfortable as they each ran to the toy that first grabbed their eye. The rest of us sat at a small, blue round table with tiny bright red chairs that fit perfectly with the table.

The woman spoke with my parents for only a few minutes and then called my siblings over to join us. I sat there with my arms crossed making it as well known as I possibly could that I did not want to be there. Matt and Anna were asked what their favorite colors were, the games they liked and if they would join the woman in playing with Play-Doh. The woman finally acknowledged me and, in a demeaning voice, as if she was talking to a child, asked me, "Would you like to play with Play-Doh, too? It's lots of fun." I don't think I could have given her any more of a stubborn look. What was she thinking talking to me, a fifteen-year-old, like that? I was not a child, nor did I consider myself an adult, but I certainly did not appreciate being talked down to, especially from someone whom I was suppose to trust and confide in.

We were scheduled to go back again and I was not thrilled, to say the least. I didn't feel like being asked to play kid games by someone who really just rubbed me the wrong way. I knew the day we were suppose to go and purposely stayed after school as long as I could with extra help, hoping I would miss my family going to the session. I was quite disappointed when they drove towards the school as I was walking home and picked me up. Once again the woman talked to me like I was ten, asking mostly yes and no questions. I didn't mind because I was only willing to share that much anyway. I guess my parents didn't like their experience there either because, to my liking, we never went again.

It wasn't too long after we stopped going to counseling that my parents brought us to someone else. I didn't think counselors could get any worse than the previous one we had seen. I was quite wrong. We only went once to this new counselor as she only made my parents fill out paperwork and look over agreements. She kept asking them what it was they wanted her to do for them and not once did she address my siblings or me. It seemed to be a waste of time other than supporting my opinion that there are some pretty bad counselors out there. Two bad experiences with counselors caused me to never want to see one ever again and made me feel even more alone.

Our parents decided to try for a third time, only the person would come to us, in our own home. I was still not comfortable with seeing someone but if I had to, being in my own home was where I'd want to be. We aren't catholic but my parents had a nun visit us. This nun wasn't dressed the typical nun part in all black but rather in everyday clothes in which you would have no idea she was a nun unless she mentioned it. She was the best person of all three; she was so gentle and knew just what to say. I was spoken to differently than the way she spoke to Anna and Matt, and I appreciated the fact that someone recognized that.

Although she was a nun, she never once told us that our brother was in a better place or forced the religion card down our throats. She asked what we use to do with Chris and what he was like. She wondered what we would miss most and truly got to know us. We only saw her a few times but it was enough to restore my faith in the fact that there are people in the world that can help. She was one example of how people just happen to come in and out of your life at just the right time and with a purpose.

Say Cheese

"To take a photograph is to participate in another person's mortality, vulnerability, mutability. Precisely by slicing out this moment and freezing it, all photographs testify to time's relentless melt."
- Susan Sontag-

When our accident happened, Chris was in seventh grade and the close friends he had were passionate about doing something, anything to help out. Four of his closest friends wrote a letter to the school community asking for donations to plant a tree and put a bench in front of the middle school he attended. Friends in his Boy Scout troop worked at making the bench and placed it in the ground in front of the school. When the maple tree was planted and the bench was completely ready with a plaque, there was a dedication day for anyone who wanted to come.

Chris' friends and others said a few words and then pictures were taken of everyone putting a white ribbon on his tree. Our family was asked to take pictures on the bench and in front of the tree. I felt awkward being in a posed picture for such an occasion. Do you smile, do you frown or do you look indifferent? You usually smile for pictures, but I didn't want to be fake and make people believe for years to come that I was okay at that moment in my life. But, yet again, people really did believe that I was "okay" at that time. I was always trying to prove that I was strong enough for everyone. I am the oldest and was made to believe that I had to take care of the two siblings I had left and anyone else who needed me.

Members of our community were always saying how great it was that I could take care of my siblings and be there for them because I was quite a bit older. People would comment and ask how my siblings were doing, "Are they doing okay? I'm sure you're taking good care of them." I was not and I'm still not their parent and couldn't understand why others thought it was my job to take care of my siblings on more of a parental level. Their words made me feel awfully guilty and very responsible, as if I hadn't been able to protect one of them and now it was my job to make sure the other two make it okay.

I think everyone in the picture felt the same way because no one seemed to know whether to smile or not. Chris' friends who initiated this donation got in the picture as well and you could see the pain on their faces as they got closer to our family. This was not something anybody wanted to be doing and I felt terrible that these boys lost one of their best friends so unexpectedly. So what do you do when you're asked to be in front of a camera, do you smile?

Escaping To Innocence

"One of the virtues of being very young is that
you don't let the facts get in the way of your imagination."
~ Sam Levenson ~

The first summer without Chris came in the blink of an eye. The sun was hot and it shined brightly practically every day. It felt great to be out of school and just relaxing although not having much of a schedule to keep me occupied frequently allowed me to think about my brother, Chris, and our accident. It felt strange not having another sibling around to do stuff with. While the summer was filled with activities here and there it felt empty, the house felt empty. I felt empty. Despite these feelings of emptiness, I ignored the way I felt.

I met several new people throughout the summer and saw old friends that I generally only got to see during the summer. It was such a peaceful and relieving feeling to be with new people and those I had not seen throughout the school year. Many wouldn't know what happened or, if they did, they wouldn't know that I was the girl it happened to. At least I thought they didn't know. I was in for much more than I had expected when I found out everyone I knew from the camps I had been going to since I was a baby, knew everything. People looked at me differently, with that puppy-eyed look of "Oh, you poor thing. How are you doing?" It spread like wildfire; those who hadn't known now knew from others who talked and filled them in. When I disclosed to a new friend what had happened to me within the past few months, they had responded with "Yeah, I know, so-and-so told me." As long as I stayed in my hometown or within that area, I wouldn't find anyone that did not know "my story."

Although they knew what had happened they had not heard it from the one who experienced it, me. Soon, friends were asking me what *really* happened. People wanted the details that they had been too shy to ask about earlier on. I never had a problem with people asking questions. In fact, I welcomed it and still do. It made me feel like people cared enough to go out of their way and ask a very important question. That meant they *wanted* to hear me, they *wanted* to listen to the answers; and they accomplished both their questions as well as facilitating the forward motion in my own grief process, without me even realizing it.

At the two-week summer camp that I was a teen helper for, I met both a couple with four children, all considerably younger than me, and a boy, Ryan, just a year younger. Tasha is the eldest of the four children and would help me out when I babysat her and her brothers often. I connected with Tasha immediately as she reminded me of myself when I was younger, helping all my babysitters and Mom with my siblings. Her bright and youthful personality brought me back to the life I had before I became the girl who lost her brother.

Spending time with her and her brothers lifted my spirits and, for the time being, while I was with them it took the pain away. Their giggles, smiles and love for play brought innocence and peace. It made me incredibly happy to see another family, much like my own, still intact and have such zest for life. Within the few months we had met, and in the years to come, Tasha and her family had instilled and would continue to instill strength within me, starting from my core. Tasha's mom was, and still is, so kind and warm. I found comfort in her presence and the way she spoke to me as an "adult" although, at fifteen, I was probably still merely a child in her eyes. While talking to me the way I wanted to be talked to, she never made me feel overwhelmed with adult-like responsibilities; I could still be a teen. It was with those who made me feel as an equal that I took the most comfort.

Ryan, the boy I met, was extremely sweet and always took my feelings into consideration. As our friendship grew he was so supportive and always forgave my outlandish behaviors and words, which at times I know hurt him. Ryan would show me what it meant to love and care for someone wholeheartedly. There were times I felt like giving up on myself; it was partly because of him and the constant push of love he gave me that I did not give up. It makes me wonder about the rest of the people in the world; there are not that many out there who forgive because they graciously want to, giving others the chances they need.

Lingering Presence

"Recall it as often as you wish, a happy memory never wears out."
- Libbie Fudim -

Growing up, my siblings and I were so very fortunate to have a backyard in which you could play and imagine just about anything a child could want. The backyard where I grew up has several fun things including a 24-foot round pool that is four feet deep, and a beautiful wooden playground with a tire swing and bumpy slide. We have a wooden clubhouse raised above the ground about six feet, which my dad built himself, and a sandbox underneath it. We thought it was the coolest thing to have a "Dad-built" clubhouse in our very own yard and we used it frequently. A few years before Chris passed away, Dad put a zip-line in, starting up a tree and ending at our clubhouse. This was one of our favorite toys. Chris and I were always trying new ways to make it more thrilling than it already was.

Back by the perimeter of our yard, we have a decent sized natural pond in which there are fish, frogs and some crayfish. Chris and Frank used to spend hours by the pond trying to catch frogs and store them in a small, blue plastic baby pool. They had no plan for the frogs; it was just a hobby of theirs to catch as many frogs as they could. The pond is surrounded by several different small bushes, forget-me-not flowers, and tall, purple wildflowers. Cattails are in different places within the pond and will quickly take it over unless managed on a regular basis.

One of my favorite parts about the pond is its location, underneath large branches of an eighty-foot pine tree with a small white, cement bench to sit on. After Chris passed away, this place brought an enormous amount of serenity and it was right in my own backyard. It brought back several memories of Chris and Frank climbing the pine tree to get away from "the girl" during the summer, and ice skating or playing hockey on the pond with my siblings during the winter.

The yard seemed to have lost its innocence and fun after Chris was no longer around and it took a long time to adjust to that change. I could find Chris everywhere in the yard, just not in the same way I remembered before the accident. Memories of him would echo in my head as I looked around the yard. If I closed my eyes, I could actually see my brother laughing and gliding down the zip-line with such ease. The memories felt so real, which they are, but somehow, when I opened my eyes it was as if none of it had ever happened. Not only would I have my past memories to remember him by but also a small yet significant gift that, from that summer on, would remain rooted in our yard.

Family friends had given us a beautiful, small weeping willow tree in honor and memory of Christopher. They planted it towards the back of the property, about twenty feet in front of the pond, to the right. It is a beautiful weeping tree that blossoms every year with small white flowers. It was planted in honor of his life but, more importantly, as an expression of the love that we had and would continue to have for my brother, as it grows.

Losing Sight of Me

"You fear that if you lower your guard for even one second your whole world will disintegrate into chaos."
- Douglas Coupland -

Chris' birthday is July 20th and this particular year, only five months after he died, would be the first time we did not celebrate his life. He would have been thirteen. Matt's birthday is July 25th and we continued on, having the annual birthday party which we used to have for both brothers. Except this year it would just be for one. How do you just stop having birthday parties for someone, especially when it is a child that you never expected to stop celebrating with? It felt strange but the pain was bearable because I had another brother to celebrate at the exact same time. So it appeared as though nothing had changed.

Shortly after Matt's birthday my parents decided to try one last time bringing me to a counselor, by myself. I was unaware of their plans and anger rose quickly inside of me when I found out an appointment was scheduled without asking me. I don't know why my parents thought I needed to see a counselor on my own; I think they were concerned that I wouldn't heal in a proper and healthy way. What I do know is that it pushed me so far in the opposite direction of where I needed to go that the little progress I was making for myself no longer mattered.

I went to the first counseling session; Dad introduced me and left. I was, as before, stubborn beyond belief, mostly because I was being forced into it. I was as resistant as possible, sitting on the opposite side of the room and answering as vaguely as I could. I was doing it purposely, not because I didn't trust the counselor, which I did not, but just to spite the fact that my parents were forcing me to do something without asking me. I was enraged with the idea that my parents thought I was the only one in our family who needed counseling. *What about them?* I thought. *What about their grief?* I seemed to remember that when others suggested my parents see a counselor as a couple or on their own they responded defensively and were almost offended. So what made them think I was "classified" as someone needing to see a counselor? And how come I couldn't make the decision myself? What separated me from my other siblings, being a teen?

I thought the counseling would stop after I "tried" it once for them but Dad continued to take me. The counselor never made me feel like a child or demean me in any way. I just did not feel like talking, especially after my parents chose to take me to this particular counselor. I didn't open up until the counselor found a soft spot of mine, music. I was asked to bring in some of my favorite songs so we could listen to them. The fortress I had built around me was beginning to crack as I explained what the songs meant to me and why.

It wasn't long after I had just barely created a foundation with the counselor that Dad stopped taking me. He told me that he and Mom did not like the counselor anymore. I never found out why, but it caused me such confusion and again I was backtracking in my grief. I couldn't understand why they had taken me to a counselor against my will and then decided not bring me back, again without asking me what I thought about it.

I began to lose a lot of my hope, the love I felt and the joy of just living that kept me going. What was I here for? Nothing made any sense to me and everywhere I turned there were people doing or saying something that irritated me. I didn't know who I was anymore. After losing a loved one, the idea of living without them is unbearable; all I wanted to do was be with my brother, wherever that was. And it's difficult expressing those feelings to anyone, especially as a teen, because the first thing anyone jumps to is the fact that you're suicidal.

All I wanted was for the pain to stop and I thought heavily about what it would be like to "live" with my brother. I wondered what it would be like to not actually live, and what my brother felt as he slipped away from consciousness. I never thought about taking my own life but I thought if I shared that I wanted to be with my brother, where there was no pain, others would interpret that as me wanting to kill myself. So I kept it all to myself, slowly spinning downward with no sounding board to bounce things off.

What do you do when you have lost your way, when all hope seems to have diminished, when you begin to live life in such a robotic fashion just to get by? What happens when that one grain of sand for light no longer gives you the strength to push forward? For me, I tried so very hard to keep it shining; it took every ounce of me to keep up what little strength I had and whatever was left from my bright personality. I no longer could do this alone, that was certainly a fact but how would I manage when I felt like I had no one? People were dropping off my support radar left and right. The few months of summer were turning me into someone I had not wished to be and I had to figh it.

Beacon of Light

"Sometimes our light goes out, but is blown again into instant flame by an encounter with another human being. Each of us owes the deepest thanks to those who have rekindled this inner light."
- Albert Schweitzer -

Before Chris passed away our church had casually started looking for a youth leader, until August when the church received interest in the position by another pastor. Kathryn Kibbie Laird became our youth pastor after she found us. Kibbie, as she likes to be called, is a beautiful, spunky and bright woman who lightens every life she enters. Having Kibbie become a part of our church and a part of my life was one of the best gifts God could have given me at that point in my life.

Kibbie made a point to visit every youth's family and have dinner with them. I felt so special and important that she took the time out to get to know us. I was extraordinarily drawn by her personality and soon found myself wanting to share everything with her. I had found an adult that I so desperately wanted to have a connection with and so I took a chance at trust. She would take me out for lunch or dinner every other week and I found myself disclosing more and more each time.

The words came with ease as I told her, "I lost my brother this past February in a car accident." She listened so intensely, every once in awhile adding a comment about what it might feel like. "It feels like someone just hit you in the head with a sledge hammer and you just can't seem to find the balance to stand back up," she said. It was like she knew and felt exactly what I was thinking and feeling. "Yes!" I said with enthusiasm, yet wondering how she knew so well. She continued, "I know, because I lost both my parents in my early twenties." Finally, someone who knew what it felt like and actually wanted to share with me.

Kibbie became one of my closest friends within the blink of an eye as we continued sharing with each other what it has been like losing someone we love. I had no trouble sharing with her, even my most deep feelings, and I began to feel like I had gained a couple more sand grains, which brightened my light. She rekindled my fire of strength. I took comfort in her words as she expressed what it felt like for her then and now. I also took comfort in knowing that one day my future would become like her hopeful and inspiring present. Although we didn't lose the same person, Kibbie brought an enormous amount of relief, hope and restoration of faith back into my life.

In meeting Kibbie, I was given a foundation to build upon my grief, a platform that I could now stand on and a first step to climbing my way out of the ominous, dark hole I had dropped into. It was as if God had sent her to me at my most desperate moment, to jump into the hole, hold my hand and lead me to light. There is always one person that walks into your life after the death of a loved one that gives you hope of surviving. That was who Kibbie was for me; she saved my life. Kibbie definitely saved my life.

When you meet new people you have no idea what kind of affect they will have on your life, but when I look back on the times I spent with those I met during the summer of 2000 and the amount of love they showed me, I thank God for having them in my life. I saw hope in my future. It had been very small but it was still there. It was as if I had begun to live a whole new life, leaving the one I had behind. I wish it had been as simple as that, to just leave it all behind. I would soon find out that would never be the case as there would be constant reminders of what happened.

The Power of Cookies

"Friendship doubles our joy and divides our grief."
~ Swedish Proverb ~

Once school started, routines had been made and I was in the swing of things. I had realized that I was not as okay as I thought I was. As school progressed, I watched my grades begin to slip. I didn't put the effort into my classes that was needed to maintain my B+ to A average and they dropped to Cs and Ds. Normally I would have cared enormously about my grades dropping, but I just did not care, at all. Teachers would tell me that I needed to do better but I really couldn't have cared less.

I loved my biology class, the information was incredibly fascinating to me but the work I had to do for it was at the bottom of my priority list, as was most other schoolwork. I was in danger of failing the class and my teacher explained that all I needed to do in order to pass the class was hand in my labs on time. I didn't study for my tests and would generally get low 70s. I think she knew I could do better but all she wanted from me was to be able to pass the class. "Do whatever it takes to hand in those labs on time and you'll pass," she said. I had no motivation whatsoever and had to find something that would push me to get my labs in on time. They didn't have to be perfect or even somewhat good; they just had to be submitted on time for me to pass. I could do that, right? *Just push yourself,* I would say. *You know you're better than this.* I think that little pep talk worked for one lab.

Lunchtime was, by far, one of my favorite periods, but whose isn't? I loved it because it was my time to try to enjoy life, to laugh and smile and to appreciate the people around me. Oh, how I would just love the time I spent with friends and the things that made me laugh. These were the times I had relied on to get me through the day, the night and into the following day until I could have it again. My favorite things to get were a bagel with cheese and their hot cookies. No matter how hard I tried to make the bagel with cheese at home, I could never get it to taste as good as the school's.

During one of the lunch periods, my friend, Lauren, and I started talking about our bio class. Lauren was always a great student and wondered why I couldn't just simply turn my labs in on time. I honestly did not have an answer for her other than I just didn't care to do the work. It wasn't that I didn't want to pass or that I wanted to retake the class; I knew that was what would happen if I didn't do it, but I wasn't thinking about the long term. The two of us were on line for food and I realized I didn't have 75 cents to get my cookies. Lauren offered to buy them for me and I told her I would pay her back. "You know what, Michelle," she said, "don't pay me back. From now on, for every lab you hand in on time I will buy you your cookies." Buy me my cookies? She had said the magic words!

From then on, I had made it my job to purposely hand in my labs on time and it made me feel so good to have them done, knowing that I was guaranteed better grades than I was getting before. I was proud of myself for handing everything in on time and the cookies were a much-needed bonus. When I received my first grade, it was higher, although I had expected it to be much higher. I found myself disappointed and somewhat discouraged, so I asked why I didn't get a better grade. "I told you if you just handed in your labs on time you would pass the class, not get an A. If you put more effort into it, I promise it will show in the grade. You can do this, Michelle, I know you can!" my teacher exclaimed.

I found myself calling Lauren often, making sure I completed the lab correctly and was pleased to see my grade indeed had improved. Slowly but surely, just my biology grades were beginning to improve. Lauren never backed down on her agreement and I always got my cookies as long as I could hand in my labs on time. Who would have thought cookies would have been such a powerful motivator? I'm not so sure it was just the cookies that made the difference. It was a friend who saw me in need of help and made it her business to help me, who believed in me enough to buy me those cookies each time I did something that would benefit my life.

If only I had Lauren in all my classes! Not having her in all my classes was okay because she gave me a small dose of what I use to be like, of what

I wanted for myself, and she started a spark that I would eventually ignite into a fire. Improving my grades was something only I could do but I could have never pointed myself in the right direction without the sincere help of a loving friend.

El Accidente

"The trouble with using experience as a guide is that the final exam often comes first and then the lesson."
~ Anonymous ~

It took an immense amount of effort to concentrate in my classes long enough to even remember what was said each day. It was even more challenging to concentrate when words or phrases were mentioned that reminded me of my brother or of the accident. When I was reminded, it was as if my mind took me right back to the second I learned of Chris' death or the few seconds I remember being in the car.

I remember my Spanish class being one of the most tormenting classes when we got to the road/car unit. We were learning all the words for road rules and the names of each type of vehicles such as car, ambulance, fire truck, van, and bus. Spanish was one of my favorite classes as well as one of my best. I enjoyed learning how others said the same thing just in a different way. I had done okay in this class until it came to the test for the road/car unit. I was prepared for the information on the test but certainly not prepared for how the test would be formatted.

I received the two-page test and began answering what words stood for "left" and "right" in Spanish. About half way through, the test turned into a story and I had to fill in the blanks with the correct words. In Spanish, the story began with explaining a car accident. We had to know what vehicles would come to the rescue after someone was injured, or after the car went on fire. The word "accident" sent shivers down my back and all I could hear were the screams of my own accident. Crashing sounds were resonating in my head as I tried to complete the rest of the test. Why was this happening to me? I tried my hardest to push it out of my head but the thoughts and images were stamped in the forefront of my mind. The bell rang and I had several blanks on my test.

When my grade was returned to me I looked at it with anger, not so much for the low grade of a 60 but for the fact that I could have done just fine if it weren't for what happened to me. It wasn't until then that I realized the trauma I had been through even if I had not lost my brother. Everyone wanted to talk about the loss we all had so much that I never really had the chance to evaluate the trauma of the accident itself and I wouldn't be given that opportunity until I went away for college.

This was not my best work and I knew that, so I took the time to visit my guidance counselor, Mrs. Reed. I entered her office and just dove right into everything I was feeling, explaining as much as I could remember in one sitting. I shared with her my Spanish test and said I could have done better if the test did not revolve around an accident. She spoke with my Spanish teacher and I was able to retake it, doing much better than I had on the first. I knew it wasn't healthy that I couldn't even take a school test without having some sort of a mini flashback but I refused to ask for further help.

Not asking for even just a little bit more help, I believe hindered my life in high school. I enjoyed the fun times I had with friends and I was usually always laughing or smiling, because I truly wanted to but it could have been that much better if I had only asked for help earlier on when I really needed it. Asking for and admitting you need some more help was something I would learn later on as true strength, not weakness.

Forgotten Griever

"To the outside world we all grow old. But not to brothers and sisters. We know each other as we always were. We know each other's hearts. We share private family jokes. We remember family feuds and secrets, family griefs and joys.
We live outside the touch of time."
~ Clara Ortega ~

As a sibling, you see every aspect of your brother(s) and/or sister(s). You see how they act in front of other people, the way they carry themselves around the house and you pretty much know all the things they do that your parents will never know about, whether good or bad. For all those who have siblings, you know what it's like to have a connection with them, even if you aren't close. Spending your every day, early life with them creates who you are and, in most cases, you cannot remember life without them. It's a very strange feeling to wake up one morning only to remember you had lost something, someone you had known your entire life of remembrance.

The first year without Chris was a tremendous struggle for me and my other two siblings as far as grieving. I can remember throughout the year and immediately following his death, my parents were the ones who received most of the acknowledgement for the loss. Cards would come in sympathy for the loss of your child or son. When people wanted to know how "we" were doing, they were always referring to our parents. Or when an adult friend of mine was talking with me, the first question they would ask in reference to the loss of my brother would be, "How are your parents doing? Are they doing okay today? I'm sure you're helping them out and helping with Anna and Matt."

Rarely was I ever asked how I was doing with the loss of a sibling. And if it wasn't my parents that people were asking about, it was my two other siblings who were both younger than ten. I heard family members and others express concern for Anna and Matt because they were so young. I had been mentioned in conversation but only to make it known that I was not of too much concern because I had a lot of friends. That's the reason why I shouldn't be of too much concern, because I had many friends? Although I had several friends, not many of them took the time to really listen to me; they had no idea what to do or say when I brought my brother up in conversation. Why would they? They were only fourteen and fifteen like me, with no traumatic experiences under their belts. If it was not me but one of my friends who had lost a sibling in high school, I don't think I would have known what to say or do either.

In the midst of the world trying to remember my entire family, I had felt forgotten. I know others thought of me and were genuinely sympathizing but I had still felt forgotten. And maybe it was partly because my brother left me; he forgot about me and our other two siblings. How could he leave me in such pain? I was angry with him for not trying hard enough and at the same time felt overly guilty for thinking that way. *Who gets angry with an innocent person whose life was taken away from them?* I thought.

I was certainly confused at who I should have been angry with. Maybe it was God I should have taken it up with or the entire world. I was full of anger, even for myself. *How could I have not tried harder to turn my head in the van when I heard him scream?* I began to feel responsible in some small way for not being able to help him. I was upset and angry with anyone I could think of *but* the man who had caused the whole thing. I had wondered why someone could do such a thing but I never placed anger on him. Should I have? I don't know. Somehow I felt more at peace not holding it against him. So what happened to him, the one who caused me to lose my brother? I'm sure you have been wondering.

Forgiveness

"Forgiving does not erase the bitter past. A healed memory is not a deleted memory. Instead, forgiving what we cannot forget creates a new way to remember. We change the memory of our past into a hope for our future."
~ Beverly Flanigan ~

October of 2000 my parents went back down to Maryland for the trial of the man who had hit us back in February. The information concerning him and our accident would be revealed, at least to me. My parents knew most of this information within a day's time of our accident but I had not been included until after they returned from this Maryland trip.

Before our accident, this man, whom I'll name Roger, had been up for an open bench warrant on several accounts such as assault, theft and failure to appear in court. When we were hit, he ran from the scene because, according to him, he was scared and knew there was a warrant out for his arrest. A K-9 unit was dispatched and found him several hours after the accident about a quarter of a mile from the scene. At that point, his blood alcohol level was at least 0.10 and he was escorted to the same hospital we had been sent to.

After being detained, he was charged with a DWI, fleeing a scene, eluding the police, vehicular homicide and several other charges. During the investigation, police found drugs in his apartment and a large 40 oz. bottle of opened beer on the passenger side of the van he had been driving, which he had taken without authorization. My parents went to his trial and watched as he admitted to everything. Roger apologized to my parents, telling them if he could take it away, he would. It was never in my parents' nature or personalities to hold wrong doings against others and hold anger for them.

My parents taught me what true forgiveness meant after Chris died. They held no resentment or anger towards Roger and made that well known to all their family and friends. Dad told me it was not his responsibility nor place to decide what ultimately happens to Roger. So if it was never in his hands, why should he live the rest of his life in anger when there was nothing he or anybody could do?

Forgiving is not only something I was taught but it sets you free from the anger and purposely takes it out of your control. Not being able to truly forgive someone for their actions and tightly holding onto the hate and the grudge can and will take over your emotions, your life and ultimately toy with your sanity. It slowly takes away the love and joy people have, eventually killing it, without you noticing how or when it died. I think it can be hard as humans to look at forgiveness as being that simple. It is not easy to "let go" or set free the anger, hurt, resentment and hate you might feel towards someone who wronged you, especially when the first thing you can think of is to somehow take revenge and give them what they deserve.

Roger received seven to eight years in prison without probation. Even after everything he had done, he got out on good behavior after just under two years. Not long after being let out, Roger was into the same habits he had been before he had taken a twelve-year-old boy's life. How is it anywhere near fair when a person takes a life in such a situation, gets out, and then continues their bad behavior? It is far from easy to forgive someone who obviously is not truly sorry for what they did. If it were sincere, people wouldn't intentionally repeat their hurtful behaviors, knowing what the outcome could be.

It doesn't really make sense to me, what some people do, but if I had not forgiven him I would have been harping on these facts for the rest of my life. I didn't want to live a life filled with hatred and anger because of what happened to my family and me. Forgiveness goes a very long way if you'll let it, remembering that just because you forgive someone never means you forget what was done to you. It truly is a gift to human kind, if we would take the time to open it.

So what does forgiveness mean if it doesn't mean to forget? Kibbie once said that forgiveness is used when we simply cannot forget. It starts with giving up the right to retaliate, then moves forward to not allowing the wrongdoer to consume all of your thoughts. Thirdly, as Kibbie explained, when you forgive, you stop seeing the person as "the one who did me wrong." Instead, you begin to see them as another human being who might be lost, who hurts just like you, and, lastly, forgiveness ends when you are able to wish the person well and not hold anything against them. This, forgiveness, is extremely hard to do but well worth doing for the sake of your own sanity and happiness.

Dear Chris

"Siblings are the people we practice on, the people who teach us about fairness and cooperation and kindness and caring - quite often the hard way."
- Pamela Dugdale -

I had several emotions flying around all over the place, too many to be able to remember all at once. I could never remember everything I wanted to say when Kibbie and I had our lunchtime. I found great relief in speaking with her but there was no way she could be there for every moment I felt something and needed to talk. We got on a discussion about who our loved ones were to us now that they weren't with us.

I hadn't thought about the relationship after he left. In fact, I hadn't thought it was possible until she asked. She continued to share how she thought her parents were her biggest cheering section in heaven. I was asked if I ever thought about my brother as someone who watched over me and if I ever thought about talking with him. She told me if I wrote to him as if he was away in another state and told him everything, how I felt, and what was going on, it might ease the transition of having no communication.

I listened to everything she had to say while thinking to myself, *I'm going to write to a dead person? How strange.* The more I thought about it, the more it made sense. I had *so* many things I wanted my brother to know; why not write to him? I knew he would never actually read them, but somehow it broke my pain up to be more manageable. So not long after our conversation, I began my first letter. I first told him how much I missed him and how life had completely changed since he left. I wrote to him about what it was like at home and how sorry I was that I had never said I love you. I shared all my regrets and finally divulged what was going on in my life at that time; school, friends, family and the boy I had liked throughout high school.

Although Chris and I fought, as all siblings do, not many knew that we confided in each other for the personal things that went on in our lives. He would ask what to do with friends or girls that he liked and I did the same with the guy I thought was cute. If ever one of us had been crying, the other would make sure our face had not shown signs of it by taking a wet towel and dabbing the reddened areas. Chris was always there for me when I cried. Having a brother close in age definitely had its advantages and it was great to exchange advice with a boy I could always trust. But having a brother close in age also meant having the worst of fights.

There were times when I just wanted to wring my brother's neck and vice versa. I will never forget one of our worst fights, in which we had turned it into a wrestling match. Chris was so angry at what I had said to him, he blew up and began attacking me. Although I was just as angry, I couldn't help but laugh at the expressions he was making and found it hard to defend myself. This only fed his anger more and I found myself lying face down on our living room floor with both my arms behind my back. I figured this was the extent of the wrestling match since I was pinned to the ground but Chris was not happy that I continued laughing at him. "You think it's funny?" he asked with an irritated, raised voice. Before I could even answer him, I felt a sharp pain in my mid-back. He had raised his elbow and slammed it into my spine.

After I got the wind knocked out of me, I screamed bloody murder. It felt like he had actually taken a knife and plunged it into my back. I was on the floor in great pain with tears rolling down my face. When the pain subdued enough to stand, I got up screaming at him. I expressed how much I hated him. At that moment, I had wished for him to have the worst pain or at least what I had just experienced. I made it well known to my family and friends for quite some time that I hated him.

After Chris passed away, for well over a year, one of the only things that ran through my head was, *You told him you hated him*. I thought maybe his death was my punishment for hating my brother in that very moment and admitting it to him. Did I really mean the word 'hate'? Did I even know the strength and meaning of the word, being so young? No, I don't believe so, but it ate at my heart and my soul to think about the words I had used, knowing my brother was no longer here.

Why is it that when someone we love passes away, we automatically think of all the negative things we did and the positive things we did not do? It's these memories we let consume us with guilt and even more frustration then we already have. It's hard to tell yourself that you were a good sibling when all you can think about is the time you told them you hated them. Although a very painful memory now that he's no longer here, I would have given anything just to be fighting with him.

I wrote to Chris in that first letter apologizing for any hurt I had caused him and that I hoped he'd understand that I hadn't really meant I hated him…I was just angry. I wished I had said "I love you" but I wished even harder that I hadn't said "I hate you." I learned later on that loving your sibling(s) is a constant even through the anger and not actually saying "I love you." If it had been me who had died, I would certainly have known my siblings loved me even though they had never said it to me. So why shouldn't Chris have known the same? The letter was ended with an appropriate,

Love,
Michelle

First Christmas

"The soul would have no rainbow had the eyes no tears."
-John Vance Cheney -

After Chris died, the holidays became a blur. I cannot remember any of the holidays the year he passed away except for Christmas. I have no memory of what it was like to not have Chris around on Easter, the Fourth of July, or Thanksgiving, but that first Christmas I remember as if it occurred yesterday. Christmas has always been my favorite holiday. I love the atmosphere and the beautiful decorations. The music is heartwarming and there's something about walking inside to a sparkling, lit Christmas tree with a star or an angel on top.

Every Christmas Eve, Chris and I would talk about what we thought Santa would actually bring us. Waking up on Christmas morning was always my favorite part of the holiday. It wasn't the gifts that got me excited; it was Chris running up to Anna's and my room to wake me up. He would shake me until I opened my eyes. "Michelle, get up, the presents are here," he would say with an excited smile. He wouldn't leave until I followed him downstairs. Our tradition was to sort out the presents before anyone else woke up. We took all his gifts and put them in a pile, all Matt's gifts and put them in his own pile, and so forth.

Christmas of 2000, the first without Chris, was the most painful holiday I have ever experienced. I woke up that morning to the sounds of my family downstairs around the tree. They had all gotten up before me and there was no Chris to wake me up early enough to sort out the presents. The second I opened my eyes, I knew what day it was. I knew there was no way of skipping it and there was no way around the excruciating pain I was feeling. I closed my eyes and felt the warm, salty tears fall down my face onto my pillow. I had no will to get up and soon my family had realized I still hadn't come downstairs.

Anna and Matt came racing upstairs to get me up. "Come on Michelle, get up, the presents are downstairs," they both said. The words caused my heart to tighten and the tears just wouldn't stop. "No, I don't want to," I replied. Matt was six and Anna, ten. They couldn't understand why their sister didn't want to get up to open presents. In fact, they were quite frustrated because Mom and Dad told them they couldn't open anything until everyone was in the living room. They walked downstairs slightly irritated and reported to our parents what had occurred. "She won't get out of bed, do we still have to wait?" one asked.

My parents were in my room next and sat on the edge of my bed. "Why don't you want to get up?" they quietly asked me. I shrugged my shoulders. I knew if I explained myself and admitted out loud that I missed Chris, I wouldn't be able to stop crying. "Do you miss Chris? It's okay to miss him," they told me. I couldn't even answer; the tears just rolled off my cheeks, soaking my pillow. All I could do was nod my head yes. My parents assured that it was okay to miss Chris and it was okay to cry. They left me alone in my room and encouraged me to come downstairs when I was ready.

I could hear the sounds of a happy family on Christmas morning and I wanted to be a part of it although my face showed an enormous amount of pain. It is incredibly hard to force yourself to join something fun or happy when all you want to do is cry and all you feel is pain great enough to last two life times. That Christmas, I will always remember as my most painful holiday, but every year it gets that much more livable. Of course, when you're in your worst pain you never believe you could feel any better nor do you think it could get any worse. I chose to get out of bed that morning for one reason only as I thought to myself, *Now is as good of a time as any to embrace, at the same time, what I lost as well as what I have waiting for me downstairs.*

A journey begins with a single step; a common phrase we can all relate to in life to remind us that it doesn't matter what pace the journey is at, a journey is a journey as long as you've made the effort to go. But you could begin to walk or run for miles and truly, sincerely, not want to be there. It's just a bunch of footprints. So are you really going anywhere without your heart in it? While taking that very first step is a milestone in one's journey, it only begins when you *choose* it to; when in your heart of hearts you say, "*I'm* going to do this, I may not know where it'll lead me or how long it'll take but *I'm* going to do this." Then and only then does the real journey begin.

I could have very easily walked downstairs, numbing my emotions and telling myself, *This is a piece of cake, keep walking.* But I knew going down there would be painfully difficult and challenging. If I was going to embark on a journey, it would be the real deal. No numbing aid, bandages or tear suppressant, just pure, raw emotion waiting to pour out of my body. I sat up in bed, swung myself over the edge and said to myself, *I'm going to do this.* My feet were planted on the floor and I began putting one foot in front of the other. I may have been wobbly, but I had chosen to do it, which was good enough for me.

Distance Between the Earth and the Moon

"A sibling may be the keeper of one's identity, the only person with the keys to one's unfettered, more fundamental self."
- Marian Sandmaier -

Adjusting to the loss of a sibling is an incredible life challenge. Adjusting to any major loss is a life challenge. When you lose someone in your life, you change, you become a different person, there's no doubt about that. Whether it's a small or large change, people notice and sometimes make it known that they've noticed. Some might say, "You're not the same 'Joe' I knew last year. What happened to you?" Is there an answer to that? And what do they mean you've changed? You're still the same person. But then when you sit down and think about what people have said, maybe they see the facade you unintentionally put on while trying to be the "same" person you were before the loss, hiding the pain. And then you come to realize that in trying so hard not to lose who you were, you have in fact changed.

Sometimes you lose more people in your life because of one major loss. You've apparently changed so much that friends begin to drift away. It makes it even harder when you've just begun high school and friends are already coming and going without a tragedy. Those who walk with you even after enduring such a sudden change are truly the friends you want for the rest of your life, but it doesn't make it any less painful for the ones that were lost along the way.

The biggest change I saw in myself was adjusting from being the oldest of four siblings to the oldest of three. The years between my siblings and

I when we had all four of us only seemed natural. I never saw my sister as being almost six years younger than me, nor did I think of Matt as being ten years younger. I never saw this because I had a third sibling, Chris, in between us, making the gap not look so large. After we no longer had Chris around, the space between Anna and I seemed only comparable to the distance between the sun and the moon.

All of a sudden Anna and Matt were no longer just my siblings; they became children to me. How was I, at fifteen, supposed to relate to what the two of them were going through at five and nine? It was hard for us to find common ground. We had lost the same sibling but our processes would all be completely different. Anna now became the middle child and because of the larger gap, I had felt like I was an only child. What was then happening in my life always seemed so far away from what my siblings were doing in their lives. If Chris were still around I would have continued making a connection with a sibling who was doing similar things as me.

When Chris passed away, I had lost not only a sibling and friend but also half of whom I identified myself with. Chris and I were always able to do things together that our younger siblings couldn't participate in because of age, maturity, height, etc. Anna still had Matt and Matt still had Anna, and my parents had each other. I lost my buddy, someone to relate to, half of myself, and I felt very alone. Chris had always been a part of my memorable life. I remember what it was like to not have Anna or Matt around but I have no memory of life without Chris until he died. For a long time I felt quite out of place in my family without my brother, Christopher, because I saw everyone still having their "buddy," their "other half" beyond a death.

Although it was a great challenge to find my place again, I am certainly glad I had and have two other siblings to remind me of Chris and to continue having memories with. What if it had been just Chris and me? My heart weeps for those who had only one sibling and lost them. I can only imagine how great a challenge and struggle that would be to never have another sibling in your life, knowing you did at one point. And what about those who have lost their twin? The adjustment of sibling repositioning, whether you become the youngest, middle, oldest or only child after the loss of a sibling, is heart wrenching and, quite frankly, it goes without much recognition. Why?

The Battle Field of Grief

"The Sorrow which has no vent in tears may make other organs weep."
-Henry Maudsley -

Winter had set in and all the greenery had turned to bright white with a thick blanket of snow from the recent storm. It was bitterly cold outside and the wind only made it worse. Matt, Anna and I chose to go outside and play in the backyard with our dog, despite our bodies alerting us that this was way too cold. The snow was so heavy that it was snapping some of the thickest branches off of trees. I looked over at Chris' tree, which appeared to be engulfed in snow other than its trunk. The branches that once wept elegantly were now stuck together by thick ice and cocooned under a foot and a half of snow; it looked half dead. The weight put on his tree was causing it to sag and you could anticipate that if it wasn't helped, it too would start losing its fragile limbs. The three of us brushed off all the snow and gently picked off what ice we could, as we watched it slowly lift back to its original form. We certainly lightened its load as it was just barely carrying its own weight, but this would be a cold and very hard winter for all of us.

Grief is such a funny thing; just when you think you're done with it or through some of the worst pain, it starts all over again. The one-year anniversary of Chris' death came within the blink of an eye, yet every day felt like time had slowed down purposely to torture me. Had it really been a full year? I didn't want it to be; the more time that had passed meant the further I went away from my past and the times I had spent with Chris. Moving forward in time also meant that there would no longer be any more new memories with him. Did that mean I'd slowly forget everything as time progressed?

When the anniversary came around, I had felt somewhat disappointed with what little friends of mine had remembered. It was never their responsibility to keep track of the days or how long it had been since *my* brother passed away. Everybody seemed to want to help and be involved immediately following the accident but it seemed like friends didn't want to be bothered now, when the world had forgotten what happened. I clung to those who had remembered that day, trying to go about my everyday routine. I purposely shoved my nose in my books whenever I could. I knew that the very second I stopped the routine or disrupted it, I wouldn't be able to function properly the rest of the day.

I fought back my emotions the entire school day. I was bound to fall apart at some point. I had to stay after for extra help, so the halls were real quiet. Afterwards, I packed my bag with the books I needed, closed my locker and started to leave. When I lifted my head, I met eyes with Frank and another close friend of mine, there at the end of the hallway, both knowing the day would be hard. I saw them both, the way they looked at me, and lost all strength I had forced myself to have throughout the day. I immediately dropped to my knees at one end of the sophomore hallway, crying as much as my eyes would allow at one time. I began hitting the tile floor with my fists in anger and my friends grabbed my hands and wrapped me in their arms, rocking.

I was angry that I had to go through this all over again. *Doesn't this ever stop?* I wondered. *Doesn't the pain ever stop?* They held me until I had no more tears to cry in that moment. I had felt so much all at once and so extremely that I caused myself to become numb again. I took a deep breath, feeling relieved I couldn't feel the pain in that second. It truly is amazing what the body does to protect itself when it knows it's had enough. This was a fact; my body, my mind, my heart and my soul had enough.

Sweet and Sour 16

"Kind words can be short and easy to speak, but their echoes are truly endless."
~ Mother Teresa ~

The anniversary of Chris' death also meant that my birthday was only days away. I was turning 16 and asked my parents if I could have a sweet sixteen party. We had planned it for months and several of my other girlfriends were having them; it was the big "thing" to do that I was unaware of until I experienced a sweet sixteen myself. I felt guilty for wanting such an elaborate party and knowing it would be fun. Chris was only gone a year and now I'm celebrating? Not only celebrating but I'm going to enjoy myself. I kept thinking to myself, *You are so selfish and heartless for wanting to have a good time.*

The party was absolutely beautiful and I had my hair done by my favorite hairdresser. The day could not have seemed anymore perfect. I had all my family and closest friends in one room. I felt absolutely wonderful and at the same time completely miserable that Chris wasn't there to enjoy it just like everyone else. The music was booming, the people were dancing, and I went to get food along the buffet line. A friend came up to me and told me how nice the party was and began to confirm what I had felt and told myself earlier.

She continued on saying, "So I'm surprised that you had a party or that you're even celebrating your birthday, seeing as how your brother died around this time." She spoke as if she was telling me that the food was really good. I was so taken aback by the comment; I didn't know how to respond. I just finished getting my food and returned to my seat, thinking of what she said for the rest of the party. Now somebody else had said out loud how I was feeling. Did that make me selfish and heartless? I never told anyone what my friend had mentioned to me that evening. I assumed everyone felt that same way. Throughout my party, I had wondered what was going through each person's mind. *Does he/she think I shouldn't be celebrating my life too?* I wondered.

My thoughts continued after my party as we brought all my cards and gifts home. I had appreciated everything that was given to me although it all felt empty. I thought about whether people really wanted to give me these gifts and whether people had even cared it was my life I wanted to celebrate. I was alive and my brother was dead; I felt guilty enough for that, I did not need others to escalate or validate that feeling.

The cards read, one after the other, "Happy Birthday, Happy Birthday, Happy Birthday." These words just felt like something you say once a year; they had no meaning to me anymore and I didn't want people to think I was ungrateful. What does having your birthday really mean? It should be about celebrating the life that was brought into the world, appreciating and acknowledging what that life has done and will continue to do in the future. It's about taking a day out of the year to thank a life for who they are and the difference they have made in your own life. If you think about all those who have made a difference or an impact on your life, without them, your own life would be very different; celebrate them for that.

One of the last cards I had opened was from my friend Dominic. I had expected what most other cards said although when I read it, the ice of bitterness towards life that surrounded my heart began to melt. The card read, 'It's more than just your birthday, it's a celebration, too…for after all, it is the day the world was graced with you'! Ironically, the gift he gave me was a beautiful, scented blue candle called Soothing.

Again I was given a light, a flame when I needed it the most. Without him knowing it, Dom had shown me it was okay for me to celebrate myself, even when others may not have thought so. Nobody thinks that it's their words, their gestures or simple facial expressions that will have such a profound influence on another's life; it can happen! It can be your words, your thoughtfulness that changes a life and, in fact, it's usually always those people who think they did something so insignificant or nothing at all, who make a very large difference. It's those little things you do that will take another's life a very long way.

An Empty Seat, An Empty Heart

"When someone you love becomes a memory, the memory becomes a treasure."
~ Unknown~

Soon after the one-year anniversary, my family and I took our yearly trip down to Florida…in our new van! "Was it too soon to go?" most asked me. I actually thought it was the best thing our family could have done. If we hadn't gone like we normally would have, who knows how long it would have taken us to get back in a vehicle and drive all that way.

It didn't bother me to be in the car, on the same trip our accident had been on. I was more worried about feeling left out, now that we were missing Chris. The trip seemed to be going rather well while I kept myself busy playing the games Anna and Matt wanted me to, until it was the day for Disney. We had gone with just our family and, as we walked throughout the park, I began to feel very alone again and robbed of something I knew I could've had.

Matt and Anna were too little to ride anything Chris and I would've, so asking my other two siblings wasn't even an option. The only other option I had was to ride with either Mom or Dad. Although they each said they'd go on with me, I had to pick and choose the rides I wanted to go on most because Mom and Dad weren't going on everything. The more I saw that had changed from our previous Florida trip, the more my heart sank, lower and lower to the ground. I knew that if Chris were here I wouldn't have had to choose only certain rides because he would have been the one pulling me on all of them. We had just so much fun on the rides together and our joy could have been enough to fill the state of Texas. Never did I ever think there would come a day, so young, where I'd be saying goodbye to such joy. How true it is that we don't know what we've got until it's gone, and how hard of a lesson it is when you lose it.

While experiencing several rides and attractions with my family, without Chris, was incredibly hard to do, it wouldn't compare to the way I felt when I had to sit by myself on a smaller roller coaster my whole family could go on. We were on line for the ride and it didn't really faze me that I would probably be the one sitting by myself, until it was our turn to wait on the platform for the roller coaster to return. None of us thought about who would sit with who, it was just a natural reaction for everyone to take their normal spots. Anna took Matt's hand and went to a row, Mom and Dad went to a row and I went to a row.

We all jumped in, excited about the ride, and I soon found myself stuck—stuck in a two-seater car with my two siblings in front of me, my parents behind me and nobody next to me. I wanted out, desperately, but knew that wasn't a possibility as soon as the train slowly crept away from the station. It was gut-wrenching, heartbreaking and, quite honestly, the longest roller coaster ride I have ever been on. It was the first roller coaster I had to ride by myself since Chris died and I wished for it to be the last. Deep down inside of me, I felt him there, next to me, with his hands up and a bright smile on his face. Somehow, that made it a little more painful, to feel he was there with me, though I couldn't see him, and I couldn't hear him.

Some of my most painful memories after Chris died are those of things which I use to do primarily with him. Nobody could replace the emptiness that surrounded me while I did some of our most favorite things without him. It's rather difficult to continue on with what the two of you would normally do, only without the person you so dearly love; sometimes too hard to bear.

Some activities Chris and I use to do together, I quickly put a stop to only because it hurt so badly to do them on my own or with other people. It was these activities that I locked away in my vault of memories to be cherished only by me. Other activities I had refused to give up purposely because it kept my brother close at heart. Riding thrill rides, especially roller coasters, was one of our loves in life. Continuing to ride them was my way of honoring that passion he had while enjoying it myself, which meant we were still sharing the memories, the experiences, although in a very different way. Now, at every theme park I go to, I dedicate the last ride, privately, in my heart and mind, to my brother, Christopher, with my hands up and a bittersweet smile.

The Horrible, Rotten, No Good, Random Day

"If pain causes no fear then it will have no power."
- JJ Dewey -

Life had really begun to change. I had experienced a full year without my brother and instead of guessing or wondering what certain, important days might feel like, I thought I'd be prepared from then on, on what to expect. Although I would never again be blind sided on what it might feel like to not have my brother around for holidays, birthdays or special occasions, I was unaware that I could feel something completely different than the previous year, on the same day.

When the pain is no longer a daily, constant feeling, I hadn't expected to hurt just as badly on random days, for no apparent reason other than it just hurt, badly. Some days I just woke up hurting and others I had been just fine until something so simple reminded me of Chris. When reminded of him, I was reminded of what happened and the pain of not having him around. This would always be a packaged deal; I could never be reminded of one and not the other.

It irritated me that something so average, something that I could see every day could send me into a whirlwind of emotions. The Nacho Doritos that a friend ate for lunch or a phrase someone randomly said would bring me right back to the times these reminded me of my brother. It felt incredibly stupid to cry or get emotional over Doritos and nobody would ever understand how a chip could cause someone's day to take a turn for the worse. I wasn't even sure myself why it hurt so badly, but it did.

Chris used to eat the original Doritos so much that I swear his darker complexion was due to the orange pigment of the chip. It was his all time favorite chip and he could "smell it out" when Mom had hid them somewhere in the house. He was always asking me to indulge in the big bag of chips with him, most times I would. I ate them so much while Chris was around that the smell and thought of eating them now makes me queasy. After Chris was gone, Doritos were very rarely found in our house and I missed that.

On these random days, all I wanted to do was crawl back in bed, under the covers and snuggle something, anything, that brought comfort at that moment in time. Random days are difficult because you don't even have the comfort of knowing that others know the day will be hard for you. Your random, difficult, painful, sometimes torturing day is just another day the sun rises and sets for those you know. Nobody knows you're in pain unless you tell them, unless you admit that there's something wrong when someone asks, "Are you okay?"

Telling someone you're not okay, that your day has been nothing but painful can be a challenge, as it opens a door to feeling more pain. Doesn't it always seem to be that when others ask us "what's wrong?" we become immediately vulnerable to that question, finding it difficult to hold it all in? We push people away for that very reason; for fear that the pain will come pouring out. Everyone wants the pain to go away. I wanted the pain to go away.

The only way through it, the only way to lessen the pain, is to feel it.

Good Will Come of It

"Listen to the mustn'ts child. Listen to the don'ts. Listen to the shouldn'ts, the impossibles, the won'ts. Listen to the never haves, then listen close to me... anything can happen child. Anything can be."
~ Shel Silverstein ~

After experiencing such a loss, I could never understand why people would always tell me, "Good will come of it." The phrase irritated me to no end. How could *good* come out of the tragic death of a twelve-year-old boy? How could my brother's death bring any sort of *good* to my life? I don't think people realized how absurd that phrase sounded as they were trying to comfort me as I grieved. Sometimes, you just want, no, need others to wallow in your pain and confirm that life couldn't get any worse.

There's a time and place for the inspiring "things will get better" speech and it's not when you're feeling some of the worst pain. And how exactly are you suppose to respond to those comments as you're crying and your chest feels like it's caving in? When people tell you, "Things will get better, don't cry," it's almost like they expect a response such as, "Oh, okay, *you* say it'll get better so let me start by wiping my tears, standing up tall and push forward because *you* said it gets better, no problem." There's a point to feeling like life couldn't get any worse; let yourself feel it. And when the time comes, there's a point to experiencing new and better things in life; let yourself experience them.

Sometime close after Chris passed away, I had joined SADD, Students Against Drunk Driving. I chose to join because there had to be something else for me to do besides sit in my room, weeping. I eventually became co-vice president and then co-president with my friend Lauren. I loved being part of the group and enjoyed the many activities and events we facilitated. It's remarkable what you can do when you get several people together behind a cause. The teacher who oversaw the club pulled me aside one day when I first joined and had shared with me, with tears in her eyes that she too lost her brother. I was comforted and somehow felt at home around her. It made some of the more painful activities easier to handle.

Once I became a member of SADD, friends and peers began asking questions about what really happened, the full blown out detailed story. People wanted to hear it from the horse's mouth and once the word spread that I was willing to talk about it, I began being asked to speak at several high school assemblies around my county about what it had been like to lose a loved one to a drunk driver. *Why do they want me to come?* I thought. *I'm just a high school student, don't you usually get adults to come and speak?* One principal said to me, "You're living proof that it happens to young people, you're not invincible and you're willing to talk about it, right? That makes you the perfect candidate to share your story in my high school."

Was I really about to do this, speak in front of hundreds of other students about some of the worst pain I've ever felt? Could this be a great thing I was about to experience in my life, something "good" transpiring from a tragic death? Sometimes you don't even know you're doing great things or that you've done something good until after you've already done them.

Speaking Through Pain

"Footprints on the sands of time are not made by sitting down."
~ Anonymous ~

I sat there with some friends from another high school, in the front row of their auditorium waiting for their assembly period to start. I was excited that they had chosen me to be their keynote speaker but thoughts raced through my head. *I hope I don't cry. What if my voice shakes and I can't get the words out?* I had always been a shy person in the classroom as well as with public speaking, although I was quite the opposite around my friends. The principal introduced me. I stood up and began sharing my story with an elevated heart rate and a shaky body. I had lost control of my nerves. There were about three hundred people in the audience and I scanned the room for familiar faces. They would be my anchor if I needed a form of visual comfort when the words got too hard to speak.

I began my story much like how I've told you, and I had done fairly well until I could feel the pain rising from my gut into my chest as I knew I had to state out loud, in public, that my brother was pronounced dead. I had never done that before but in some strange way, I felt as though a weight had been lifted off my shoulders. I think I might have lost it at that point if it weren't for one familiar face I had zoned in on. The audience would never know I had reached breaking point although never broke in half, thanks to the familiar face that grounded me. I hadn't expected the audience to listen so intently but as I scanned the auditorium I couldn't find a pair of eyes not on me and several people had been crying. I couldn't believe that what I had to say would have such a huge impact on other people, especially my own age.

My favorite part of being in front of so many people was when I stopped talking and answered questions. I loved hearing what other people had been wondering about throughout the whole story and I enjoyed answering questions. I think it truly helped me push through the process of losing Chris. Several had wanted to know what happened to the man who hit my family, as I hadn't mentioned that in the story. Others went a little more personal and asked me what I would tell my brother if I had the chance to say one last thing.

If you were asked that question about your own loved one, what is it that you would say?

The Class of 2005

"You have brains in your head. You have feet in your shoes. You can steer yourself in any direction you choose. You're on your own. And you know what you know. You are the guy who'll decide where to go."
~ Dr. Seuss ~

Being an upper classman brought several happy, memorable experiences but it also meant school life without the sibling I thought I'd always have with me throughout school. Entering my junior year, Chris would have been a freshman. There were many in my own class year that had a sibling the same age as Chris. In fact, several of my friends had a sibling in Chris' class year. It was one of my many challenges to watch as friends and other peers grew closer with their own sibling as I had to grow apart. As I watched others have what I so desperately wanted back, the pain at times was unbearable.

What was so painful about watching other siblings was that Chris and I were just getting to the point where siblings don't fight as often. We had grown just enough to experience having a civil, advice giving relationship for just about a year. I felt like something was stolen from me and at times feeling angry at others with siblings close in age. I was angry and jealous. When friends would mention, "Oh yeah, my brother/sister has this today so I have to wait for them," or "Did you know my sister/brother likes…" I couldn't help but wonder what my brother would be doing or who he'd like. I'd have to keep the thoughts to myself when I thought of Chris because nobody wanted to hear about someone who "no longer existed."

It was very hard to learn that society didn't take well to talking about a deceased person, unless it was decades or hundreds of years later and they belonged in history books.

When I walked the halls, I saw everyone in his class and several of his friends every day. I couldn't escape the loss of my brother anywhere, I "saw" him in each one of his classmates and especially in all of his friends. It was a bittersweet feeling to see them all because it brought pain knowing he would never be around the hallways himself but I felt as though all of them, collectively, brought him closer to me and kept him alive in my heart. I felt connected with them in some way and could see the pain and struggle on their faces when they encountered me.

Losing Chris was extremely hard for his class, I could see that. Most of them hadn't experienced such a loss, why would they have; they were only in seventh grade. As I began to make connections with some of his classmates and friends, I heard their own story, the loss of Chris through their eyes. The stories helped me piece my own story together and I felt less lost knowing what others had gone through at the same time I had. I watched as some of his friends began to phase the loss out while others continued to struggle with the pain.

I had heard that one girl locked herself in her room for days, unable to face the world on the other side of her door. Others experienced so much pain that they had to attend another school. I felt horrible that his death had such traumatic effects on so many people and I couldn't stop it even if I tried. One friend of his, as I walked by her in the halls, I could just sense the enormous amount of painful energy she gave off. Running into her brought up the several memories I remember of her and Chris playing together in our backyard or the fact that she had known him practically her entire life.

A few of his friends became volunteer firefighters, just as Chris had wanted to do, and continued to be a part of the firehouse even after high school. How proud I was of each one of them for doing such a great thing, no matter their reasoning. I had felt somewhat safer and didn't feel so much as if something or someone was missing knowing that others who knew my brother became firefighters. The money that people gave in my brother's name, our family decided to donate to our local fire department in memory of Christopher.

Chris' class, the class of 2005, endured the loss of my brother in which began a "trend" of losses the class would have to bear. Throughout high school they had many others whom passed away unexpectedly, causing some to experience more trauma and all to grow beyond their years as adolescents. Here's to all of you out there who have lost a friend, a loved one and your innocence because of it. Your strength shows just by waking up each morning.

Faltering Words

"Grief can't be shared. Everyone carries it alone, his own burden, his own way." ~ Anne Morrow Lindbergh ~

Enduring a loss within a family system is incredibly challenging. People shy away from each other, divorces are initiated and finalized, and everyone experiences the loss in their very own unique way. What my parents and siblings experienced, I will never know completely, just as they will never know all that I've experienced. This is what makes the loss challenging; we all lost the same person but at certain times we would all have to face what we lost on our own, in our own way and on our own time line. To make it through some of the most painful times of grief a family has to fight not only for their own way through it but for the system itself, the working body as a whole. When you lose a limb, the body or system must work doubly as hard to keep itself working sufficiently, but even more critical, to simply keep itself alive.

I watched as we all went our separate ways while living in the same house. The communication changed and it became harder to figure out what we were all talking about or what we meant by the words we had chosen. Sometimes the words we might have used were unintentionally hurtful; the words came from our own personal pain. The words that usually hurt are the words that come from those closest to us.

I had written a poem in memory of my brother and was rather proud of how it turned out. I wanted to read it to my family so I brought the scratch piece of paper it was written on into the kitchen where my siblings were sitting at the table and my mom washing dishes in the sink. After I read the poem, my sister asked if she could have it. I replied saying, "Well, you can't have this one, but I'll make a copy of it for you." The next thing I knew Mom was snapping at me for not giving the poem to Anna. She kept asking me why I couldn't just give her the poem, what's the big deal? Each time she asked, her voice got louder and more irritated.

We argued back and forth for several minutes about why I wasn't going to give my sister the original poem and then she ended the conversation when she stated how she really felt. "How come you don't care about your brother and sister? Maybe if Anna and Matt were killed too, you'd care about them then." The words went straight to the most sensitive place of my heart and took my breath away. I was so stunned that my own mother would say such a thing that I had nothing to say back. I was incredibly hurt and just walked away, out of the kitchen. I was thankful I had dance in just fifteen minutes which meant I couldn't sit at home dwelling on the words she had chosen to say out loud.

While it hurt tremendously in those moments and for many years following, as I got older I understood that it was never her intention to purposely hurt me. She was hurting just as much as I was. It's amazing the things you learn years later, which you wished you had learned in the moments it could have been useful. As a teen I had no concept of what it really meant to be married, and raise a child, let alone four. I don't think you really do until you're in it. What I did learn about my mother is that she's another human being who hurts just like me. She's a woman who just lost her son and is grieving while at the same time taking care of three other children who grieve too. She is a woman, a wife, a mother and a griever packed into one body, one mind and one soul. My parents fought hard to keep our family system together and what a long way we've all come, still being an intact family system.

I will never know what its like for my mother unless I lose a child and my mother and father will never know what it's like for Anna, Matt and I until they lose one of their own siblings. What I do think we can understand for each other is that we all do hurt, in our own ways. Not that the hurtful words we use are excused but we can relate knowing that sometimes the pain is really that bad, it's so bad that, that's all we can think about, "my pain".

It's a hard thing to accept, knowing whatever words you choose to use when speaking with someone can never be taken back. Sometimes you mean the words and sometimes you don't, either way they are forever out there. It always seems to be the hurtful words we tend to remember most, the words that bring us down and cause our heart to ache. Is that because the words cause some sort of trauma or rather because we don't hear enough positive comments from the people that surround us? It could very well be both.

Only Human

"The imperfections of a man, his frailties, his faults, are just as important as his virtues. You can't separate them. They are wedded."
~ Henry Miller ~

When someone passes away, regardless of what relationship you had with them or how they treated you and others, it somehow seems, for the most part, that they become considered a saint. They become someone who could do no wrong while they were alive and only the good things get mentioned. God forbid you might mention something not so becoming of the deceased person; it's not respectful people say. It's almost as if you've committed a sin in saying, "Well, they weren't so nice to me."

What if the person had never been there for you, letting you down for the majority of the time and hurt you often? Are you expected to attend the person's wake and funeral to praise them for all their life goals and achievements? It's not that you wanted to see the person die but that's what others believe you think when you share one or more of the person's less positive characteristics. Sometimes a person's less positive characteristics and faults are made known throughout their lifetime but as soon as they pass away they become the world's best person, regardless of what people previously said and thought.

Now don't get me wrong, I am not trying to say that my brother was anywhere near a bad person but he was far from being a saint, as we all are. He was a troublemaker in our family and loved to pull pranks on people, especially his siblings and close family. I remember many a time having Mom and Dad yell at him for whatever mischief he had been in that day.

Thinking back on all the jokes and mischievous things he had done makes me laugh now. It makes me laugh when I think of the ridiculous things we *all* did as kids. But at the time, soon after Chris passed away it bothered me that my parents didn't think he had done anything wrong; it was as if he had become the golden child.

There were times I would share a story about something he did and I would get, "Oh, I don't think Chris would have done that," in reply. Or I noticed when they wanted or didn't want us (Anna, Matthew and I) to do something they would throw in a comment like, "Chris would have or wouldn't have done it." It made me feel awfully guilty if I hadn't done whatever it was they said. I never told my parents how it made me feel, as I knew they too were going through their own process on top of trying to keep the family as stable as possible. While you're actively grieving, you don't really see beyond your own pain and journey. It wasn't until later that I truly knew that the words my parents had chosen to use were not to intentionally hurt me, Anna or Matt, but that doesn't mean it never hurt.

At times, I felt as though my parents thought I didn't care my brother was gone or even worse, that I wanted him gone because I didn't just talk about all the good things he did. Other times I felt quite the opposite, as though they thought I cared too much about Chris and not my two other siblings. I was rather conflicted on how I was supposed to feel or act because of it. Being the oldest had become more complicated than I could have imagined after Chris was no longer around.

The point is, nobody is perfect. Even those we love dearly make mistakes, including those who've passed on. What is it that makes us not want to admit that after a death? Maybe it's the power of guilt. "How could I say the not so nice things I know about? It's wrong." Or is it too painful to reflect on the bad times that we just want to erase those parts of the person's life? On the contrary, I truly believe that every life did at least one great thing for another, even if it seemed small, at one point in their life, no matter how bad or good the person's reputation was.

My brother was a great person, but he wasn't perfect and it's okay to admit that. He teased, pulled some not so nice pranks, and he hurt me at times, just like any other normal brother would be doing, just as I know I did the same to him. Just because I remember and talked about some of the bad memories of my brother, does not mean I don't remember all the good memories or that I didn't care he died.

My brother was only human. Just like me.

All In the Timing

"And that is how change happens. One gesture. One Person.
One moment at a time."
~ Libba Bray ~

Senior year of high school was filled with excitement and I thought I had grown quite a bit since freshmen year. I continued making new friends, as it was easy to do with a class size of 350, and I involved myself in many new activities I had always wanted to do throughout high school. I tried out for the fall drama and got what I thought was the perfect part for my personality.

I had an incredible amount of fun and got to know some really awesome people. Once our lines had been memorized and we were doing a run through, I had been backstage talking with two friends from my class year. We had gotten into a discussion about what it would be like to go away for college and how weird it was going to be not having all our childhood friends with us. One friend, Evan, began wondering what we'd all be like after a year away and started sharing what everyone in our grade would be like. The three of us giggled and laughed until Evan started to describe whom he thought I'd turn out to be.

Evan kept laughing as he told me that I would probably be the biggest drunk of us all. The other friend and I stopped laughing as hard and I told him that would never happen, with a slight giggle. He thought it was the funniest thing and kept going with it. "I bet you'll be the one hammered all the time, driving everywhere and trying to get to places just to have another one," he pushed further. It was no longer funny and I couldn't understand why he thought I would do something like that. Our other friend kept giving Evan looks for him to stop. She couldn't understand why he was pushing either. I was rather offended and removed myself from the conversation.

I walked down another hallway to recompose myself before I had to put all my efforts into being someone else on stage. Our mutual friend must have said something to him because he came around the corner looking for me with such a heart-broken face. He sighed and said, "I am so sorry, Michelle. I honestly had no idea what happened to you." I told him it was okay, if he didn't know, he didn't know. This was certainly an eye opener for me, for I had thought *everybody* at least knew about what happened to my family. Here was a guy, in my own class, grew up in the same town and hadn't known what happened. I couldn't decide whether I was more surprised or relieved that there was someone in my own grade who hadn't known.

Later on in our rehearsal, Evan had asked me to share with him everything that I could remember about what happened, leaving out no details. I was taken back by the fact he wanted to know everything he possibly could about the accident, about what it had been like to lose my brother. Most people would have said they were sorry and left it at that. I was actually excited he asked to know more. It was extremely rare that I got to share my story in its entirety. All my friends knew about it, so there was no purpose in them wanting to hear it all over again.

Evan sat there listening so intently, as if the accident had just happened yesterday, while I described as much as I could remember in that moment. He stopped me at various points to ask questions. It really was a wonderful feeling to have someone really and truly want to know exactly what happened without me asking if I could share it. Sharing and telling my story with others has been an enormous therapeutic tool over time. I found that the more I shared and the more I talked about it, the easier the pain and the thought of not having my brother around became.

Evan had given me that chance, as I hadn't been able to find someone who didn't already know the story. As odd as I thought it was that he didn't know anything, he was meant to not know. Sometimes we find out about someone's loss far after the fact and it's an awful feeling to know you weren't there when it happened because you would have been if only you had known. But would you have been as attentive to the person six months to years later if you had known right when it happened? Maybe some people are not meant to know, purposely to be there when the rest of the world seems to have faded away. Evan was that person for me. He gave me that outlet in that moment in time just by wanting to sit there and listen. Not only that, but Evan not knowing helped me transition into a new setting of where nobody would know my story at all, college.

Languages of Apology

"We achieve inner health only through forgiveness- the forgiveness not only of others but also of ourselves."
- Joshua Loth Liebman -

I shared with Evan what it was like to come back to school with everyone staring and how I finally snapped at that one male classmate who simply asked, "Are you okay?" Still, after three years I couldn't believe I had been so nasty and never apologized. I thought I'd have to live with that for the rest of my life, as three years later seemed too late to apologize. The guy probably wouldn't have even remembered, but it bothered me, and my thoughts were being consumed with the fact that I never said I was sorry. I hadn't told anyone about this incident and I was relieved when Evan said that he couldn't blame me for what I said because I had just been through a huge tragedy. He also told me that if it was really bothering me that much, talking with the boy would help, regardless of whether he had remembered or not.

I finally got up the courage during my senior year to talk to the guy. I began, "I'm not sure if you remember what happened to my family and me freshmen year…" He replied saying, "Of course, I remember, how could I not?" I felt comforted in just this first response alone. It relaxed me, knowing that the conversation wouldn't be the harsh words back towards me that I thought I deserved. I asked him if he remembered what I had said to him that day I returned back to school. "Yes," he said simply. My heart sank; I was somewhat hoping that he had no recollection of the hurtful tone I had used with him.

I continued the conversation, "I am so... sorry for what I said and for the tone I had used with you." I explained how I felt that day and how everyone kept asking me the same question over and over again; he had just happened to be the last straw, causing my patience to crumble. I wanted him to know that I was not normally like that and I hadn't meant to hurt him. He answered my concerns. "It's okay, you were going through a very rough time. I knew you weren't like that normally." Although I will always remember the way I treated him, my conversation with him lifted a tremendous amount of weight off my shoulders. Because I treated him like that, I don't think he'll ever know what it actually meant to me that he even asked if I was okay, and that's my own fault. In fact, there were so many in our class year that did small things that made my life that much better, I could never share them all, but be thankful for the class I grew up with.

I learned that it's never too late to apologize for something you did even if the person doesn't accept it. Sometimes when contemplating about apologizing, one might think it makes no sense to apologize if the other person won't forgive you, especially if it was so long ago. That was how I felt. *How could this guy even begin to accept my apology after I waited so long to say anything?* I thought. Even if this boy hadn't been very accepting of my apology, I still would have felt a weight lifted because I had forgiven myself. Forgiving yourself is much like forgiving another, sometimes more challenging as you are your own worst critic.

Best Laugh

"I love people who make me laugh. I honestly think it's the thing I like most, to laugh. It cures a multitude of ills. It's probably the most important thing in a person."
-Audrey Hepburn -

Ever since my brother died I had dreaded senior year for one reason only, senior sibling pictures. Every year the school takes pictures of the seniors with their sibling(s) who are also in the high school. It was like taking my heart to a paper shredder every time I thought about it throughout my four years in high school. Because my other siblings were so much younger than me, I wouldn't be included in the senior sibling pictures now that Chris was gone.

The time had come and I knew the yearbook would be taking the superlative pictures within the next week as well as the senior sibling pictures. Frank and I were nominated for best laugh, as well as two others and we had to be in the front of the school at a certain time to take the pictures. I was fairly excited that I was one of the seniors picked as having best laugh, and what made it even better was Frank had gotten it too.

All the seniors whose picture needed to be taken were gathered outside in the front of the high school and I was thinking about how we should all pose to portray "best laugh" when the photographer asked for all seniors who had siblings to step forward. Every horrible emotion you could feel, I felt it all right in that moment. It was as if Pandora's box had been opened and it all flew straight for my heart. All I could think about was the idea of death taking my brother, how angry I was at him for not trying hard enough and jealous at those who still had their siblings and could take a simple picture. I felt excruciating pain and hated the fact that I no longer could have what others seemed to be taking for granted.

The only way I knew how to let it all escape my body was to cry a million tears. I turned away from the sibling scene and the tears began to fall. To others my tears had seemed so random; nobody put together that I should have been in that picture with Chris. This meant that I had to announce it, to say it out loud. My friend, Janine, had been standing with me and immediately came to my rescue, wondering what could possibly have happened just by standing there waiting for a picture to be taken.

After I explained to her what happened, she sighed and wrapped me in her arms. Her shirt was drenched with my tears and I wondered how I was ever going to be able to take a picture looking the way that I did with puffy, red eyes, wet cheeks and a tired looking body. This was certainly not the look for best laugh. Janine knew this as well and began telling me jokes to make me at least smile. She brought up past memories that would at times have us rolling on the floor with laughter. Our stories, the memories that we made never failed to make me laugh, even at my most trying times.

As I'm giggling and sniffling at the same time, Janine stopped the stories and put her hands on the edges of my shoulders. She looked at me and starting speaking. I could tell by the look on her face that she really needed me to hear what she was saying. "I know this has got to be very painful and I want you to tell me all about it but right now it's my job, as your friend, to make you smile for this picture, the way that everyone remembers you." The other girl in the picture with us had taken notice to my puffy eyes and asked with concern, what was wrong. I felt her arm come around me as she took me to where the picture was being taken. "Don't worry, we got you," she said to me.

I opened the yearbook in the last week of high school and saw the picture that was taken. It appeared to look as though I was laughing incredibly hard at something Frank was doing. Whenever someone would flip to this page, they would be reminded of the laugh I had. Whenever I flip to the very same page, I'm reminded of a classmate who did such a comforting, yet simple act and a dear friend who made sure I would be remembered that way, for best laugh. A friend who knew it would be hard to get in front of a camera and appear as if I was laughing, after feeling quite the opposite. A friend who at the bottom of Pandora's box, brought hope that I still had laughter. And I'm reminded of a friend who, quite honestly, gave me that superlative title by making me laugh so much no matter what mood I was in.

Laughing gives you the confidence you need to know that everything is going to be just fine. It causes me to believe that I'll stand tall even when I'm feeling rather small and I'll laugh even if it hurts to but most of all, I'll smile because even at life's worst, even if I really don't want to, it makes things that much better. Laughter really can be one of the best medicines in life, if you'll let it. It's easy to push laughter aside when you're feeling terrible because you're just not in the mood. Don't stifle it if it tries to ignite. Laughter keeps your heart happy and your soul at peace.

Gifts of All Sizes

"A double blessing is a double grace."
~ William Shakespeare ~

The moment I watched my little brother Matthew take in the tragic news of his older brother, I knew he would never have an older brother again. He had two older sisters who might help ease the pain minimally, but he would never have that older boy role model in which he looked up to so very much. While I worried for both my siblings, I knew Anna had me, as an older sister to relate to. I was always trying my hardest to include Matt in the things I did, as well as bringing myself into his world and playing the games that he'd always liked. While I did my best to be both an older sister and "brother," I could never replace the bond Matt had with Chris or give him what he could get from hanging with other boys. It's because of one family, one boy, who gave that opportunity back to Matt.

Throughout my time in high school, I had known and become very close with a family from church. Chris and I use to get together with Amy and Phil quite often. Chris and Phil were the same age, and Amy and I only a year apart. We were always having some sort of fun with each other, at times it being girls against boys in teasing matches. Amy was someone I could vent to about Chris when he got annoying and Phil was that person for Chris, as well as I'm sure it was the other way around for both Amy and Phil.

After Chris died, of course everything changed. I was now talking to Amy about the pain I felt and how I would do anything to get my brother back. While I still had Amy, Phil had lost his buddy. I could see the pain on his face whenever I'd come to hang with Amy. I knew that feeling of missing Chris and feeling left out because he was no longer around. Most of Chris' friends, short of Frank and Phil, had found it too painful to associate themselves with my family or me. This fact alone was painful for me because I found it more comforting to be around his and our friends. I felt it kept Chris alive, if they didn't drift away, it was less I had to lose.

Phil, Amy and their parents did everything in their power to help our family out whether we needed it or not. Amy would invite me places with her, involving me in events other than in my own town. Although only a year older, she taught me a lot about life and what to expect within the next year because she had already experienced it. I knew what social events to expect and the workload I'd have in school because she prepared me for it all. Being the oldest means figuring things out mostly on your own, as you don't have anyone that's been through it before to guide you. This made me feel safe with Amy in every way possible.

Phil would go out of his way to see how we were all doing, paying close attention to Matt as he no longer had his brother. Some weekends, he would purposely call to make a play date with Matt, inviting him to come play at his house for the day or he would spend an afternoon at our house. Matt loved Phil and very much enjoyed the fact that Phil wanted to play with him. As Matt's older sister, I deeply appreciated the fact that this middle school boy took the time out of his busy schedule to play with a five-year-old all the way up until Phil left for college. He gave Matt a gift, the gift of brotherhood. While Phil never replaced Chris, he made sure that Matt still had a connection with those who would be role models for him.

The love this family gave to me and my own family came at just the right time in my life and I felt relieved knowing my siblings were left at home with someone like Phil when I myself left for college. Phil gave me a beautiful light tan, soft, teddy bear when I went away for college and told me it was for me to hold or squeeze whenever I got lonely and missed Chris. Even if I spent my whole life thanking people such as this family for what they did in my life, it could never compare to the amount of love that was given to me or to the enormous amount of gratitude I'll always feel.

"I am responsible! Although I may not be able to prevent the worst from happening, I am responsible for my attitude toward the inevitable misfortunes that darken life. Bad things do happen; how I respond to them defines my character and the quality of my life. I can choose to sit in perpetual sadness, immobilized by the gravity of my loss, or I can choose to rise from the pain and treasure the most precious gift I have – life itself. I am responsible!

~ Walter Anderson ~

Left Behind

"What we have once enjoyed we can never lose.
All that we love deeply becomes a part of us."
~ Helen Keller ~

When you leave home for the first time it can be a bittersweet feeling. You're all too excited to be on your own making decisions for yourself, but there's just no place like home, whatever home is and means to you. Mine was family, old friends, my backyard and home cooked meals! Right before I left, I took a picture in my mind of my own backyard, how I remembered it as a child and how it had changed over the years. Chris' weeping willow had grown some, changed some and weathered a few years of four seasons, yet looked just as beautiful as when it was put in. The branches wept elegantly towards the ground and swayed gracefully when the wind came through at the end of August. It was always so full and alive looking during the summer. I took this mental picture to remember that whatever changes at home, the people, the scenery, colors and decorations in the house, this was one thing that would forever be the same in its place, Chris' tree.

The college I chose to attend was just about five and a half hours away from my hometown, still in New York, and I had decided to major in dance and psychology. My goal was to become a dance performer. I was incredibly excited to be going away, to meet new people, see a new place, but especially to be where nobody knew my past. I would be in a place where I'd just be Michelle without the tag of "the girl whose brother died." I could do or say anything I wanted and nobody would know anything about what had happened to me. I felt amazingly free, free from everything I felt pigeon-holed into back home. It was a much needed break from the constant loss I felt being in high school.

When I met new people and they asked me if I had siblings, I could say "yes, I have three," and describe them all without any further question as to why I'm mentioning someone who died. I could talk about Chris and the things we use to do as if nothing happened. People would know me, for me, before the fact that I had lost my brother and I thoroughly enjoyed the time of having people not know, while it lasted.

The freedom felt incredibly great for several months, until I began to miss my brother with every fiber in my being. I looked around to find comfort during those times, only to find that most everybody I had become friends with didn't even know I lost a sibling. I thought going away, embarking on a whole new time in my life, that losing Chris wouldn't be much a part of it. While the loss of Chris at home would never continue in the same way at school, it was a completely new set of "grief rules" and feelings I had never felt before. College brought on a whole new aspect to my grief. I was learning a lot about myself and what happened at much more of a rapid pace than I expected.

I found myself wanting home, terribly, for the fact alone that everyone just knew. I didn't have to say anything on days they knew would be painful and here, away at school I knew I would be forced to share that part of my life if I wanted to find comfort, if I wanted people to really know me. I thought I could be *me* without the loss of my brother but very quickly found out that losing Chris was a very large part of who I, in fact, became.

Neverland

"If you carry your childhood with you, you never become older."
- Abraham Sutzkever -

I would have to start telling people about my true past and some of the most gut wrenching heartache I went through if I was going to find comfort or face the reality, my reality, that my brother did, in fact, die; there would be no way of getting him back. I took a chance and exposed the deepest wounds I had to whomever I felt would listen. Some, as I worriedly expected, began to drift away after knowing what I lost, and others became much closer to me.

I was afraid of losing my friends for the very fact that they might be uncomfortable with the idea of me having such a major loss and not knowing how to "act" around me. Although painful to lose friends that I had an enormous amount of fun with, I knew that true friends would stay with me no matter what my past was like. I also found it hard to really connect with friends because while I loved having fun and being crazy, my loss had caused me to grow well beyond my age. It was difficult relating to most of those my age, and so those I gravitated to seemed to always be older than me or with a little more mature mentality than whatever age I was at.

Sometimes feeling older, feeling more mature than the average, caused me to be at times, bitter. I was bitter because I didn't want to be more mature than those my age. I envied them for their youthful thinking, the child that allowed them to do whatever it was they wanted or say whatever it was they were thinking without wondering what would come afterwards.

Once you've crossed over that line between Neverland and what becomes your daily grind, the reality of life, it's difficult to bring yourself back there in order to save all the imagination that you never had the chance to use. No matter how much older or more mature I would get, I clutched to my suppressed inner child through Disney. Without fail, the moment I walk through Disney's gates it's as if the gates themselves magically absorb as much adulthood as possible out of me, leaving the mature, pain felt, traumatized me on the outside of those gates.

Trauma makes us grow much quicker than we ever expect or want. I hated this fact. I hated everything I went through and how none of what I felt was going away. How could being 300 miles away from home, away from the essence of my brother not make everything at least slowly disappear? After a loss so great, you come to realize, no matter how far away you take yourself from where your loss took place, and not being around such painful reminders, the loss is still there. The pain and the trauma are all still there as you come to understand that you are a part of your loved one's essence and they are, in fact, a part of yours.

Comfort in Chords

"I get by with a little help from my friends."
-The Beatles-

The fun I had in college with my friends was an amount no words could describe. I loved the time I spent outside of studying, hanging and laughing at whatever little things we found funny. My friends kept me young, as young as I could possibly be and I loved them all for what they unintentionally did. They were always pulling me out of my shell, a little bit at a time, causing me to experience things I never had the courage for in high school.

My freshman year of college, some friends had convinced me to play my Fender Strat (the electric guitar I had at the time) in front of all my friends and others I had never met. Music played a very large part in my grieving process as it allowed me to feel in a way that nothing else could give me. Since I was young, I've loved to play music. When I saw an instrument I wanted to play I put my heart and mind into learning how to play it. Whatever it took, I would teach myself how to play. I learned how to play the violin at ten and later on decided I wanted to play the flute. My music teacher told me the flute was too hard and I'd never be able to play it after learning a string instrument. So what did I do? I taught myself how to play the flute, eventually getting first chair in one of my high school bands. I taught myself the piano and, finally, the guitar.

I had always loved the guitar but never had one to learn on or anyone to teach me the basics in order to get started. About three years after Chris died, I had gotten close with two of his friends, both musically inclined.

In fact, one had played the trumpet at his funeral. I spent so much time with them, having adventures and heartfelt conversations that I wished I'd have done much earlier in our friendships.

The summer before I left for school, the three of us, including both their families went up to one of the family's summer vacation homes. There, in a quiet, little house along a beautiful lake in the woods is where one of my friends pulled out his guitar and taught me, with such excitement and patience, the basics on how to play the guitar. The three of us had bonded in a different way up by this lake, a bond that only music could bring together. I learned rather quickly and we soon found ourselves in a small band; two guitars, a drummer, and all three of our voices.

It came quite easy to me, how to put words and music together on the guitar and I spent most of my free time composing music, just as my friends did. We kept playing well into my college years, loving every minute of it. Both taught me how to let go, to release my pain and all other emotion into music. It was as if my body was harboring all the negative emotions, and by playing with my two friends I had opened a channel for everything to flow out, bits at a time. I felt enormously better after composing or hearing a song in its entirety with everyone having a part. Losing Chris affected all of us and it showed within the songs we composed.

Being away at school, these two were of the handful of people I missed most from home for the very fact they allowed me to feel whatever it was I felt through music. Not once did they tell me it wasn't good or "let's not use that one." I loved coming back home to them. They both brought comfort to me just by being in the same room. Part of that comfort for me was that they kept my brother alive just by having known him. I loved that feeling of being around those who knew Chris. It was home. The two of them kept me together when I needed to be kept together. Every time I pick up my guitar to play, I'm reminded of how and where I first learned, as well as the amount of peace the guitar and my two friends brought to me.

Choices To Make

"Nothing great was ever achieved without enthusiasm."
- Ralph Waldo Emerson -

Having lost my brother because of a drunk driver made life and the loss a bit more complicated. I should say that it added a whole new level of grief. If it weren't for the fact that this was all done by someone who decided to get behind a wheel after exceeding his own limitation of alcohol, then I would have no reason to speak in front of audiences about the effects of drinking and driving. I wouldn't have to live with knowing what happened to my family and me, happens to another family in the world almost every day. What do you think the entire world would be like if everyone thought of just one other person rather than only themselves when making decisions? What would your own personal world look like?

But because losing my brother was due to a drunk driver, I would have to incorporate this fact in with the rest of the facts about his death that I didn't particularly want to be acknowledging for the rest of my life. It was a part of who I became and who I will always be as I continue to grow in grief. Talk about always having to incorporate it in my life, at school, somehow my RA found out about all the public speaking I had done in high school and asked me if I would be willing to speak again on the topic of drinking and driving.

I had a difficult time making a decision on whether or not to speak. I was afraid that now I was away from those who hadn't heard a word of my story, people would think I was a goody two shoes for speaking, especially those my own age. It's rather difficult to speak against something, anything, in front of peers. Even if it's something you're passionate about, it's taxing on your thoughts: *Well, what if people think I'm doing this for all the wrong reasons? Will they think I'm trying to ruin their fun, especially being a freshman in college?* I honestly didn't care about the drinking. People could drink as much as they wanted, that was their prerogative as it was mine. What I couldn't understand was why people even thought about driving if they were going to be drinking. How simple this concept was to me after losing a twelve-year-old brother. I learned the hard way, from somebody else's mistake, the effects of drinking and driving. I didn't want anybody else to learn the hard way, although unfortunately sometimes that's what it takes. I wouldn't even wish the hard way on my worst enemy.

After much thought, I had chosen to accept the invitation to speak at a freshman program, being a freshman myself. The program wasn't for a few months later and I had time to prepare exactly what I would say, as this surely had to be different than all the times I had spoken in high school. I wondered what my brother, Chris, thought of me speaking and if he would be "with me" before and after my nerves rose and tensed. As the time grew near, I doubted my ability to speak and wondered why I had even accepted.

Perception and the Truth

"No person is your friend who demands your silence,
or denies your right to grow."
~ Alice Walker ~

The friends you make at college soon become your family, the people with whom you confide in most. You begin to do everything with them, your breakfast, lunch and dinner, whenever it's possible. If that's not enough time to be with them, all your free time is spent with them, as if you hadn't seen them all day. What your friends decide to do, you go along with, and what you decide to do, your friends go along with. And when you're on school breaks, life seems like it's missing something important without them. Being away from your hometown, experiencing new people and places truly is a wonderful time, at least it was for me.

The difference between losing someone to a drunk driver and any other type of loss is that once people know how you lost your loved one, the subject of drinking becomes almost like a taboo around you. It's especially hard when you're in college and drinking and partying is a large part of your social interaction. Once people found out I had lost my brother to a drunk driver, nobody invited me out. They assumed I didn't want to be associated with alcohol for that very reason.

I watched my friends get ready for parties, asking me what outfit looked better or helping them decide on where they should go. I was in one of my friends' rooms on a Friday evening just hanging out with him and a couple of others when another friend walked in. "So I was invited to this party and can bring whoever," he said and then listed everyone's names in the room except mine. "Wanna come?" he finished. I looked around the room waiting for someone to wonder the same thing I had wondered. How come I wasn't invited? No one spoke up.

Could I have asked to go or say I'd go, too? Yeah, I suppose I could have and it was partially my fault for not speaking for myself whenever I wasn't invited, but it really bothered me that most of my friends just assumed I wouldn't go out because of what had happened to me. Again I was being robbed of something that every other normal college-aged student would experience.

I never particularly liked the taste of any type of alcohol when I was in college and so if I was ever offered a drink, I'd maybe take a sip or two to try it, but I would very rarely have several glasses of something, not because my brother was killed by a drunk driver, but because I simply didn't want it. And no matter what I did, even if I did end up going out a night, friends were always "checking up on me," making sure I was okay with being out. It got rather annoying and irritating after awhile because I felt like I was being treated like a child by those my own age or sometimes even younger. I guess it bothered me because I wasn't use to being babied. I was always very independent and became overwhelmingly mature after experiencing such trauma. I knew that people were only trying to do what they thought was best, but I just couldn't understand why I was thought of as being so delicate or fragile.

When having a drink, people would go as far as looking at me like I had just committed a sin and would ask or comment, "Oh, I didn't realize you're okay with drinking," as if it was dishonoring my brother's life. What does "drinking" mean anyway? Do you "drink" if you have a few here and there, or does that term only apply to those who drink frequently? Or, does it simply mean that you intake alcohol at all as opposed to being completely sober? You never really think about these things until after alcohol impacts your life in some way.

It was these experiences I had with others that kept me sitting on the edge of whether or not to continue speaking at the freshman program. I felt that no matter what decision I made, I'd always be left with the label of "the girl who doesn't drink because of what happened to her brother." Just because my brother died due to a drunk driver doesn't mean I have to swear off alcohol as the so many assumed I would and still do. This also doesn't mean that when I have a drink or two I'm trying to drown out what happened or that I am being disrespectful to my brother's life.

It's drinking *and driving* that put me in this position in the first place and ruins many lives everyday.

People speak for me when I do go out, saying things like, "Oh, she doesn't really drink," when I'm asked if I want another one and then they'll quietly, on the side, explain to the person that doesn't know, why I'm not a big drinker. Which, to them, is because my brother died because of someone who drank too much and got behind the wheel. My friends say this as if I can't hear them or if I don't know what they're doing, and for the rest of the night out everyone seems to avoid talking about alcohol around me, and it makes it more awkward and less fun.

Again I found myself just a little angry at my brother for leaving me this way, as if it was his fault people walked on egg shells around me when alcohol came into the picture. How can it be his fault? Yet, I still felt some resentment towards him for having caused this part of my life to turn in this direction. If only he was still here, I could thoroughly enjoy the time out with friends without the stress or the awkwardness of people wondering why I'm even there. If only…

Anyway

"No one can make you feel inferior without your consent."
~Eleanor Roosevelt ~

Have you ever thought about what dating would be like after you've lost a loved one? For me, I certainly wasn't thinking of how my relationships would at all be related to my loss. Dating was a completely separate entity to me. Why would losing my brother be a major topic in any of my relationships other than explaining what happened?

I didn't date too much in high school. I only had one significant boyfriend and college dating was a whole new realm. Most of my friends were guys. In fact, my very best friend at college was a guy I met my freshman year. Those who were my good friends knew all about what it had been like for me to lose Chris, including my new boyfriend who had previously been a friend. I had dated him for just about two months in which we had met each other's families, when he broke things off. Ask why. You'll never believe it!

We went for our usual nightly walk when he asked, "So where do you see this going?" We all know what this question means; either it's "I want to get more serious," or "I don't see this working." Unfortunately and fortunately in my case, it was the latter. After saying he no longer wanted to date, he started explaining in detail the reasons why. He began with each of my family members, having a complaint for each one of them. If it wasn't bad enough that he just bashed my family, it was as if he was on a roll and just led right into what was wrong with me. "You talk about your brother too much, he's dead and you need to get over that," he said. He continued with, "You only talk about him for selfish reasons, because you want attention. That's the only reason why I think you're speaking at this program for drinking and driving."

My heart could not have sunken any further as the tears rolled down my cheeks as if endless. I was upset that we would no longer be together but I was heartbroken after listening to everything he thought was wrong with my family and me. Here was a guy who seemed to think he knew everything about my family after two months of dating and meeting my family maybe once or twice. He apparently didn't like me talking about Chris, even if it was a funny story or something my brother and I use to do together, because the only time I spoke about Chris' death or my pain was when he asked me about it. The deep pain I felt when missing my brother was reserved only for talking with Frank and my very best friend at college, which should have been an "idiot light" for me to know this was someone I couldn't be with.

I couldn't understand how someone could be so cruel, so unreasonable and so unsupportive. He had made some of my worst fears about living without Chris come true. I feared people would think I did public speaking for attention and I only spoke about my brother selfishly. How could I have done speaking for selfish reasons? I was always asked to speak, I never volunteered myself. I was only trying to do some good in this world. I had just about twenty-four hours to decide whether I was going to back out of this freshman program because he broke things off the night before I had planned to speak. He convinced half of our mutual friends that I only speak out of selfish motives and that going would only support that. If I hadn't felt confident in myself beforehand, I certainly was not feeling the least bit confident in my capabilities and motives for speaking now.

Chris had been gone just about four years at this point and all the hard work and progress I made over these years had been torn down by one single person's hurtful, unreasonable words and actions. His words caused me to become bitter towards wanting to make a difference. I thought, *What's the point if so many people are only going to pull me down for the good I try and do? What's the point in having relationships if all I'm going to get from now on is, 'you talk about Chris too much'?* Even if they never say that out loud, they probably feel it on the inside. But isn't that what these people want you to think and do? They want you to think that way so that you never do it again, becoming discouraged and bitter towards the world as a whole and overall unhappy. It's times like these I'm reminded of what Mother Teresa once said:

People are often unreasonable, illogical and self-centered;
Forgive them anyway.

If you are kind, people may accuse you of selfish, ulterior motives;
Be kind anyway.

If you are successful, you will win some false friends and some true enemies;
Succeed anyway.

If you are honest and frank, people may cheat you;
Be honest and frank anyway.

What you spend years building, someone could destroy overnight;
Build anyway

If you find serenity and happiness, they may be jealous;
Be happy anyway.

The good you do today, people will often forget tomorrow;
Do good anyway.

Give the world the best you have, and it may never be enough;
Give the world the best you've got anyway.

Despite feeling unconfident, discouraged, and unhappy about where my life was at, I held my head high and chose to speak anyway.

Adam

"If you're alone, I'll be your shadow. If you want to cry, I'll be your shoulder. If you want a hug, I'll be your pillow. If you need to be happy, I'll be your smile. But anytime you need a friend, I'll just be me."
~ Unknown Author ~

While I tended to drift more towards a mature, older me, it was one of my best friends who allowed me and quite honestly forced me to be the age I was really at. Being his friend meant that most of my maturity went out the window and I could just be. If ever I felt in the slightest bad mood all I had to do was find him. I don't really know what he did but he always made it better. I felt at home with him, as he reminded me much of Frank.

I enjoyed the fact that my best friend and I only shared a few commonalities. It meant broadening both of our horizons and I loved being a part of new things. Our relationship was very different than any other friendship I'd ever had solely because we were such opposites of each other but yet somehow meshed so well. When it came to giving advice we were always right about pieces of each other's lives in which we were too stubborn to admit the other one had nailed it right on the head, so we purposely did the opposite.

He was always completely honest with me, sometimes brutally, but he would be the only one to do so. He kept me on my feet and truly thinking about the decisions I had made and would make in life. Even if I didn't want to hear it, he was always making me face my truth. He told me things that I couldn't tell myself. Oh, but sometimes his words would send me to a boiling point. Have you ever had a friend like that; one that could make it better and annoy you all in one sentence?

When I told him about Chris, I had been preparing myself to lose a great friend. I never thought he, being so goofy, would be okay around someone who felt such pain at times. "So," he said, "you lost a brother, why would that change who you are to me?" I cried in front of him for the first time and he sat there with me, not saying a word, allowing me to just be. I had never had a friend like that; and maybe he just didn't know what to say, but he didn't say that, he just sat with me so I wasn't alone in my tears.

After I was humiliated by my ex-boyfriend and felt discouraged, he came to my program to hear me speak, supporting me. He gathered a bunch of other guys on the floor to come, despite them all being friends with my ex-, and I immediately felt comforted, knowing I had made the right choice. How grateful I am for his support and the way he stuck up for his best friend, even when it meant choosing a side between all those who were mutual friends with my ex- and me.

As our friendship grew, neither of us had to say anything to know there was something wrong and I liked that I didn't even have to use words to express my pain, anger or hurt; I could just be. But when I did need to talk, he knew it and forced me to say the painful things I was trying to hide. No matter what either of us went through, he never failed to make me laugh, smile or step just beyond where I could reach. He kept "my child" alive while appreciating who I had become and gave me the chance to use the imagination, the playfulness and spunk that I thought I was slowly losing. That's why he became one of my best friends.

Life After You

"I think the thing to do is to enjoy the ride while you're on it."
~ Johnny Depp ~

I thought for sure when I went away for school that I would continue on my path to becoming a dance performer. I had been so excited to learn more, to broaden my spectrum of dancing abilities but the classes I took were not challenging and I actually didn't enjoy what I was learning. The styles were extremely different from what I had always learned and quite honestly I'm not sure I would have called these styles dance, but rather forms of yoga.

Because I began losing interest in dance, my focus turned to psychology. In fact, over the course of three semesters, I became so disgusted with the dance program that I had dropped my dance major. I could have very well transferred and chosen to continue with my dancing dream but something kept me there. I couldn't tell you what that was, but I stayed, finding myself thoroughly enjoying the psych field. As I continued down my unexpected path, I wondered what Chris would be doing and who he'd be "today." What do you think your loved one would be like today if you hadn't lost them? What do you think they'd be like ten years from now?

At this point in my life, Chris would be just around the end of his senior year of high school, waiting to go away for college or begin a career as a fireman. I make these assumptions based on who I knew he was then, though he probably would have changed, like most people do during this time in their life. Chris was very artistic and creative; maybe he would have done something with art or became an imagineer with Disney. Whatever he would have chosen to do, I would have liked to have seen him do it! While I thought about what Chris would have been doing, here I was continuing on with my own life, making plans for my own future. Life actually goes on after you lose someone you love dearly? The time ticks on, one second at a time. Sometimes, even now, each second can seem like it took an hour to pass and at times the seconds couldn't go by slow enough to even process what had happened that day.

Leaning towards the counseling field, I found myself being handed tasks, scenarios and cases which pulled me further into the field that I didn't originally intend to be in. Things began to just fall in my lap and I fell in love with the work, with the people and felt "at home" with what I was embarking on. In some ways, it's very scary when your life changes and steers off the track of what you tentatively planned out, but it was oddly exciting playing things by ear and figuring out where this ride of life would take me next. *What about if life could give me a glimpse of Heaven and a quick visit with my brother?* I thought. Now that would be an interesting "stop" in the journey of life. Could you imagine being able to visit Heaven just once during your lifetime and then return to your everyday human life? If you were able to, when would you choose to take your visit and whom would you most want to see?

Sugar Coated

"Pain is a feeling. Your feelings are a part of you, your own reality. If you feel ashamed of them, and hide them, your letting society destroy your reality. You should stand up for your right to feel your pain."
- Jim Morrison -

What happens when you lose your keys or wallet? You begin to look for them, wondering where you could have possibly left them. You retrace your footsteps to where you think you lost the item and eventually, usually, you find what you've been looking for. So why do we say "I lost my sibling" or "when I lost my parent…"? Are we in search of them not to be lost? In some ways, maybe. We search or adjust to finding a way to keep them in our lives, just in a very different way. And do we ever find them? Will we ever find them?

The concept of death and the word itself is a taboo, at least in the United States. Very rarely do we hear anyone say, "My child *died* a year ago." We've become so accustomed to being as sensitive as possible when a death occurs that we carefully choose the words we use when sharing with someone of a death. "So and so passed away yesterday," or "Mary lost her mother." Nobody ever "dies," they are either lost or have passed on. Why is it that we don't like to use the word 'died'? Is it too final for us to admit that our loved one is gone, never coming back, they're dead?

If we, as humans, could live without loss, life would be lollipops and gumdrops. There would be no pain and essentially nobody would die, including ourselves. On the other hand, experiencing pain and loss allows me to appreciate the people in my life, knowing that one day there will be life without them. Maybe that's why we shy away from using the words "they died." It's a way of distancing ourselves from the fact that we are all mortal and do, in fact, die. Even though we all know very well that's what happens, we hide from it in our everyday lives and in the words we choose to use. Ultimately it makes the loss harder because there's always a piece somewhere deep inside us that says the person never died…we just lost them.

I watched over the years the words I had chosen to use to explain what happened to my brother and how people reacted. When I said my brother "died," people were caught off guard but I could see their pain in hearing that someone had died. When I chose to share that my brother passed away or that I lost him, people were sympathetic but it was almost like that happens every day. We "lose" people every day.

Admitting and saying out loud the words "my brother died," helped me fully understand, deep down to my core, that I would never get him back. Although I think we know that our loved one is completely gone even when we use the word "lost," there's something about comprehending the fact that their heart stopped, their brain is no longer functioning and their skin is cold as ice from lack of blood flow; their body died. It's not an easy thing to think about, let alone accept.

After losing someone close to you it puts your own mortality into perspective. I realized that someday, I too would die. I've always known it in the back of my mind that my own life would cease to exist but it became a recurrent thought after I saw that my brother died. My own brother, just two years younger than me, was capable of dying so suddenly, which meant I was capable of dying at any day too.

I thought about what the world would look like if I died and if people would consider me a loss. I wondered how I would die, whenever that would be and I came to the conclusion that if I had the option to know when I would die, I wouldn't take it. If I knew when my life would end, I'd be making choices that I might not otherwise make in the joy of living every day. What I did today, was what I wanted to do in life, not in the fact of knowing I would die tomorrow. And isn't that what life should be about? Not worrying about tomorrow, or harping on the past, but living for today.? Much easier said than done, you say? Oh yes. It's something we all struggle with doing, I think. We're only human.

Although I lost Chris, and I admit I did try searching for him, to fill that void he left me with, I found him much closer than I thought I would, in my heart of hearts. For as long as I live, he too will live.

Stirring the Pot

"A new wound makes all the old ones ache again."
~ Mignon McLaughlin ~

During my time as an undergraduate, I continued learning how to live without Chris. It was most definitely a process. I got myself to a point where I thought missing him wouldn't be an excruciating hurt, and I could think about what happened, the accident, the funeral, etc., without wanting to breakdown. Losing Chris seemed, at that point, to be put at the bottom of a pot, where I'd have to intentionally dig to cause myself to feel the pain.

I couldn't understand myself when I had other losses, it brought me right back to the way I felt the week and month my brother died. It didn't even need to be another death, but if something were in jeopardy of being taken away from me, a loss of any kind, I automatically dove myself to the bottom of that pot and stirred the pain, making it rise to the very top.

Mom had been diagnosed with a benign brain tumor when I was nineteen and Dad had a heart attack just about two years later. Both received the treatment needed and recovered well but the thought of losing either one of them so young, after losing Chris was unbearable. Before knowing they would be okay, I missed Chris with every ounce of me. Whenever I had any sort of pain, whether it was after treasured friendships ended abruptly, our family dog was put to sleep on my birthday, or people I knew died, Chris was the center of all painful things. It was as if he set the bar for all losses and pain to come.

What is wrong with me? I thought. I was going through these painful events and all I could think about was how I lost my brother and how painful it was not to have him around when I felt pain. It made whatever pain or loss I was enduring doubly hard because I grieved over my current pain as well as all the pain I felt and still sometimes feel since Chris died. It made me wonder about all the future losses I'll have and whether this would prepare me for double the pain or make it worse knowing it was coming. I'm not so sure anybody is actually *prepared* for pain and loss, as if it'll make it better.

It almost made me angry with Chris whenever I lost someone/something else or it was in jeopardy because he started it; he started the agonizing pain that life would continue to bring me. I was frustrated with the fact I would never get answers as to whether Chris "chose" to leave, to let go of life or whether he fought his hardest to stay with us. I wanted to know, as this determined how mad I'd be at him for leaving and always reappearing in my life with pain. It tore me apart thinking that no matter who else I lost and whatever pain was coming my way, Chris would follow.

Hold Tight and Push Through

"If you want the rainbow, you've got to put up with the rain."
~ Dolly Parton ~

After about five years of experiencing life without Chris and pushing my way through the pain, I concentrated so much on working my way through losing a sibling that I left the trauma of being in the car accident to the side without intentionally doing so. If you've been in a car accident of any kind, even a fender bender, you know the mental effects it can have whether they last days, weeks, months or years afterwards.

For a year after our accident, any kind of sudden sounds caused me to jump or even feel as if there was an accident right in front of me. Action movies were hard to sit through as the glass shattering and cars flipping over each other took me right back to my own collision. Our accident would repeat over and over again in my head until something significant interrupted it, such as a friend really grabbing my attention to find out what our plans were for the weekend.

The nightmares I had and sometimes continue to have are excruciatingly painful. Some nights I would relive the accident over and over again, not being able to wake up, other nights I would have this one particular nightmare where Chris and I were on an intense thrill ride. How could being on a thrill ride, for me, become a nightmare? We loved them so much.

We got on this crazy ride that flipped all over the place, excited for the thrill it would give us and it began. Our laughter and small screams of fun were typical of our experience and I was enjoying myself until I realized that the harness holding us in was coming undone. He was sitting on the side of the car with the door latch and I began to panic. The door was slipping open and Chris looked at me, screaming my name to not let him fall out. "Michelle, Michelle…please don't let me fall, please," he would shout. We both began to scream out of fear and I could only hold onto him with one arm in order to hold us both inside of the car with the other arm. I couldn't really see much, everything became chaotic; lights were flashing and different colors flashed before my eyes. I held onto his hand as tight as I could as we rotated and flipped all different ways. He continued to scream for my help, but he slipped and I watched him fall out of the ride, dropping several feet into the chaotic lights and colors.

I woke up breathing heavily and really feeling like I had just lost Chris all over again, at my hands. Why was I having such horrific, traumatizing dreams? I already knew what it had felt like to hear his cry for help and not be able to do a thing about it, dreaming about it made those feelings three times as hard to have and to feel. Having these dreams really made me think and realize that I was still having a problem with the fact I couldn't turn my head in the car to help him. Because I couldn't help Chris and there would be no way of rectifying that, I began having dreams of not being able to help or save my other two siblings to the point where I'd lose them.

My dreams were very painful and very real, but at least the ones I had of Anna and Matt, I could wake up from, knowing that they were just fears trying to come alive. The ones I had of Chris, I had to wake up from, knowing that my dream had already become my reality; there was no escaping that. What I had to come to peace with was, although it was my reality that I lost Chris in a horrific car accident, it was never because I wasn't able to help him. I didn't lose my brother because I couldn't turn my head to get to him in that car. Repeating that and saying it out loud to myself minimizes the guilt and helps me know that this tragic loss was never in my hands to prevent nor anyone else's in my family.

Guilt is an incredibly powerful feeling that at times overrides all other emotions to the point where it's hard to feel anything but guilt. Because of this, because it's so powerful, sometimes it takes longer to work through than any other feeling or emotion that exists after the death of a loved one, and that's okay. In so many words, people have told me to "get over it," get over the whole thing and continue forward. The problem is, you can't continue forward if you just "get over it"; you're just suppressing it. In order to really let yourself continue on your personal journey of healing, you must go *through* it. Not over or around, but straight through. You must go through the heavy rain, snow, slush and wind to make it to the warmth and brightness of sunshine, and the newness of spring in order to really and truly appreciate them. Don't let anyone ever tell you, you should get over it. Those weather storms that you endure, that you choose to push through, make you who you are today. Be proud!

Little Message from Heaven

"Nobody has ever measured, not even poets, how much the heart can hold."
- Zelda Fitzgerald -

When I lost my brother, I had wondered if I'd ever have that feeling of truly being happy again. I'm not sure, at times, that I even realized I wasn't happy until I started experiencing the same happiness I felt before Chris had died. Have you ever had someone that brought everything, I mean everything, to life, including yourself?

I met Tim my sophomore year of college and my life took a 180-degree turn. I had been in several habits, routines and mindsets just before we met, which I hadn't realized were negative until I was around him. I had distanced myself from people and was very guarded, especially when it came to my heart. Loving someone is a wide-open invitation to pain and I wasn't sure if I was willing to invite more of that through my doorway.

Although I pushed him away at times when I felt myself becoming vulnerable, he pushed himself right back with confidence and clarified this by saying, "You're going to have to do much more than that to push me out of your life; I'm not going anywhere." Tim never once told me I was negative. In fact, he thought I was the happiest, most optimistic person he had ever met, but I had noticed it. I had noticed a change in myself and I loved it. The barrier of grief that I had built had slowly been taken down and I was okay with that. Tim became one of the largest parts of my life and I was happy to have found that a large part of life had become happy rather than tragic and painful.

I learned so much about myself after I met him, and several pieces of my life which I had purposely tried to suppress were forced to come "alive." There were many activities that Chris and I use to do with each other that became too painful for me after he died and I lost a portion of happiness because I no longer had them. Tim enjoyed much of the things my brother had, ironically, and so that forced me to allow those pieces back into my life, maybe even feeling joy from them.

My brother loved food and we loved coming up with new concoctions in the kitchen that probably nobody would ever consider to be appetizing, oh but they were. For whatever reason, cooking became a painful memory, especially around my family. I had no problem cooking for myself but when others entered the picture, I became defensive and unsure of myself. Chris was always the one who willingly "claimed" the food if our family didn't like it even though we thought it was the best thing since apple pie. Everyone that knew Chris knew he enjoyed his food and there are countless stories that made me, our family, and most of his friends double over with laughter but there are two stories, for me, that stand out and remind me of him often.

Apple pie was without a doubt Chris' favorite dessert. He begged for it at every occasion that would require some form of sweet. We were at my Aunt Jane's for one of my cousins' birthdays and she had made, from scratch, an apple pie. Chris loved Aunt Jane's food, as most others do. Our family had gathered in her living room around the time for dessert. Chris didn't want to wait for his pie any longer, so Aunt Jane brought him to the kitchen, cut a slice for him and said, "If you want more Chris, just help yourself," She returned to the living room with everyone else and when we were all ready for dessert, Chris was found in the kitchen and he had eaten the entire apple pie. Through all the gasps and sighs of disbelief, Chris had stated with his mouth full, "What? Aunt Jane said I could help myself!" Needless to say, two apple pies were made from then on, one for Chris and one for the rest of the guests. It's stories like these, which make me laugh so hard yet still, just ever so slightly, puncture my heart with a sewing needle.

Tim always listened whole-heartedly to such stories and showed interest in wanting to know more by asking all sorts of questions. Even when I wasn't sharing a story or bringing up my brother, he was. Tim included Chris in my life, like so many others hadn't. Once Tim knew the details and inside jokes of my life, he would point out the little things, the "signs," which would remind me only of my brother. It became our inside joke to point out whenever I had a bent fork.

One night at the dinner table, when Chris was around, he turned his fork sideways and clenched down on it with his teeth causing the prongs to all point inward. I wasn't sure what he was doing at the time but he had this incredibly mischievous face. When I wasn't looking he had switched his bent fork with mine and began giggling, waiting for Mom to notice that the once straight fork she had put at my place setting was now nearly unusable. As she sat down at the table, she noticed it while I was too busy trying to figure out why Chris had such a devious smile. "What happened to your fork?" Mom asked with a slight gasp. I had no time to reply as Chris answered for me, "Oh, she got hungry!" Mom was certainly not happy, but Chris enjoyed the fact that he just pulled off this "amazingly thought out" trick on his older sister.

Tim thought my brother was a funny kid, from what he heard, and always made mention that they would have gotten along. If Chris were here, he'd only be a year younger than Tim. Whenever Tim saw a bent fork he would point it out and tell me, "It's a little message from Heaven, just saying 'hi.'"

A bent fork!? It's amazing how such little things, how such everyday or random items become important in some way and hold gallons of emotions and memories encased inside them, like a cocoon. Maybe for some it's a ladybug, a butterfly or a toolbox with certain tools, and for others a certain type of candy, shoes, or a particular scent. These objects are filled to capacity with your own memories. It's almost as if they'd burst into real life if you were to try to fit one more thought, memory, or emotion into them.

A bent fork.

Beginning To Breathe

"The turning point in growing up is when you discover the core of strength within you that survives all hurt."
- Max Lerner -

Somewhere on your journey, whether it's after one year, two, five, ten, or twenty, something changes. You begin to see the world for what it is and not for the world that took your loved one. I actually began waking up each morning ready for what the day would bring, excited for the challenges, rather than wondering if this would be the day all the pain would dissolve. It's days like these, when you wake up feeling refreshed, anew, that you wonder how you got there. And then you look back, trying to figure out the day it all changed and realize there is no one day that you miraculous felt less pain.

How did I ever get myself here? I thought for sure I'd be cursed for the rest of my life with the agonizing, deep pain that came after my brother died. I looked back on the minutes, hours, days, and months that had been excruciating to endure just waiting for the next moment to pass. How quickly the time had gone when taking a glimpse of what had already occurred.

The first time I realized that I was no longer outwardly wishing for my day to be without pain, I wondered if this meant I was "letting go" of Chris. I didn't necessarily want to. I thought if I felt no more pain it would mean that my brother was no longer a large part of my everyday life. At least when I was feeling the pain, he was there, constantly following me. So when you realize you're actually enjoying life and the loss does not consume most, if not all, of your thoughts, but yet having those thoughts kept them around and in some ways alive, then how do you let go of it all knowing it'll never be like that again? I felt crazy to think, *I want the pain to stay*, because I didn't necessarily want the crying, or my heart feeling like it was bleeding to death. But not feeling that way also meant it was all "over"; the worst had come and gone. Much like not wanting to leave his funeral, I had feared what life in the future would be like without the consistency of Chris' life.

I stopped writing him frequent letters because I no longer consciously thought about having to share with my brother. It was no longer a *need* in my life. Have you ever come to the point where you feel bad, like you're doing something wrong, for not *needing* them anymore? For no longer having that constant longing to have their physical presence, even just for a second? I felt as though I had betrayed him in some way, as if I was giving up on him. What was there to give up on? He's dead. He's not coming back for me.

I wondered if your loved one knows you've begun to truly find peace; maybe not entirely, but you've begun to. And does it hurt them or relieve them to know that they aren't the center of your life anymore? We're taught that Heaven has no pain, but I can't help but wonder if he shed a tear when he left us or when he realized his family wouldn't be with him as he always remembered. What would it feel like for me if I were in his place, having to ultimately say goodbye to everyone I so dearly love? Someday we'll all, inevitably, find out.

Ending the Taboo

"When we become aware that we do not have to escape our pains, but that we can mobilize them into a common search for life, those very pains are transformed from expressions of despair into signs of hope."
~ Henri Nouwen ~

My days after I met Tim were filled with laughter and promise for a future I never thought I'd get to see. It's amazing what one person can do to really change your life, whether it's for better or worse and it's just as amazing how quickly they do it, too. In this case, Tim brought so much goodness to my life, probably more than he'll ever know. Have you ever met someone that came flooding into your life unexpectedly and became a constant source of everything good? Tim was very much that person for me.

When we first started dating, he was always surprising me with the questions or comments he made regarding Chris. I had become so accustomed to the world not acknowledging that I had two brothers, it caught me off guard when Tim actually would. I'll never forget one evening while we were at his parents' house making dinner, he mentioned something funny his brother had done. Without hesitation, I chimed in and said "Oh yeah, my brother did something like that!" Within seconds of my reply, Tim asked me, "Oh yeah, which brother?" I was completely caught off guard because Chris hadn't even entered my mind. It almost confused me for a fraction of a second that I even had more than one brother. Within that fraction of a second, my brain went from, *What do you mean "which" brother? I have one*, to my second thought, *Oh; you were actually acknowledging that this could have very well been Chris I was talking about.* I stood there, staring for a moment, which felt like several minutes until the words, "Um…Matthew," came out.

How could I have forgotten about Chris, even for a fraction of a second? It was questions like those that Tim frequently used that caused me to rethink about the wording I chose when talking about either of my brothers. The name Chris and anything that had to do with him was no longer a taboo in my vocabulary around Tim. Soon, I had found myself soaked with happiness. One, for having Tim in my life and two, because Chris was in my life, the way he should have always been after he died.

Not only did Tim make me feel alive again, bring my brother "back to life" but he was also the catalyst in meeting people around our age who also had lost a sibling. I had never met anyone who lost a sibling and at least for me, the moment I found out what we had in common, I was comforted alone in that very fact. With these two people, I never had to say one word to them about pain because I knew that they got it, they just got it. And other people certainly got why I could or would be feeling pain but there was nothing like having these two people really grasp every little bit about what it's really like losing a sibling and without saying a word. They were often around Tim's family and I enjoyed their presence while being very grateful to really know that I was no longer alone in my age group.

Tim grew up with all brothers and being with Tim for several years at this point, I had gained two more brothers closer to my age, much like what it would have been like for me if Chris were still around. They would tease me if I said something stupid or when my sports teams weren't doing too hot. It gave me a glimpse of what it would feel like to have Chris alive, being only two years younger, and enjoying what siblings do together when they are "older." Watching Tim and his brothers interact made me happy and warmed my heart. I loved seeing siblings appreciate the bond that they have. I'm not sure any of them will truly know what they've given me. All in all, the love Tim gave me and the relationship I gained from his brothers and well, his entire family will always be kept close at bay.

Hand In Hand

"There are no bonds so strong as those which are formed by suffering together."
~ Harriet Ann Jacobs ~

Seven years after not having Chris around I graduated with my Bachelors in psychology. Most of my extended family, including Tim's family, were all there. I was beside myself with excitement to have all the people I love in one place and for something so joyous. When I stood up to get my diploma, I saw my family, all thirty of them, sitting there waiting to scream for me. I scanned everyone's faces with a smile and then something snapped in my brain; Chris was not among them. For the briefest moment, it had felt like someone took a pin and pricked my chest just outside of my heart. I smiled again, knowing that it had only been a pinprick rather than a knife twisted inside me. I missed him greatly in that very second but somehow felt surrounded by his presence.

It was these moments that I thought about most when he first died, the most important moments in my life in which I'd have to experience without him. I had thought about this day years before it probably should have entered my mind, just for the very fact that I'd be doing it without my brother. As a fifteen-year-old, right when he died, I thought about my college life, the one I'd marry, the children I'd have and all these milestones happening in Anna and Matt's lives, all without Chris.

I thought being twenty-two and having seven years pass, that I would have done most of my growing and maturing when it came to the grief. Within a ten-year time span after Chris died, never did I think I'd have grown the most within the last two to three years, but I did. So much happened in those two to three years that I was forced to grow, well beyond what I thought was possible. Just when you think you're done growing, life gets thrown at you like a heavy sack of potatoes.

I got accepted into a grad school for mental health counseling and moved in with one of my very dear friends, Gena, with her husband and two little kids. I absolutely loved living with them as the kids kept me on my toes, put smiles on my face when I was feeling down and, not to mention, I had a built-in older sister and brother with Gena and her husband. I obviously never had older siblings and so it was nice to finally get a taste of not being the oldest for a little while.

Gena had been my supervisor, mentor, friend, and much like an older sister a few years before I moved in with her. Part of the reason why I chose to continue in the counseling track was from watching Gena be a phenomenal counselor; one that I had hoped to be half as good as. She walked me through my years as a grad student while I learned so much more about myself. Sometimes she walked in front of me, to show me the way. Other times she walked behind me and let me learn to take the lead, and sometimes she just walked next to me, hand in hand, when I needed to know I wasn't alone.

Being in grad school is much different than undergrad as it's much more hands-on and challenges you to take a deeper look into your own life. There's lots of typical schoolwork, but the most challenging part is learning about yourself, discovering and uncovering thoughts, ideas and feelings that you never came across before, especially in the counseling field. I enjoyed most every minute of learning but some classes really made the wheels in my brain spin much faster than I had ever experienced, particularly when it came to revisiting my own losses.

There were times when I cried so hard from missing Chris, that I thought my eyes would no longer work. How is it that so much time had passed and the simplest of discussions could whirlwind me back to those same excruciating emotions? There was one night where I just couldn't stop; the tears seemed endless and Gena came in to sit with me. I thought to myself, *What I would give to become numb again right now.* As I'm sharing my pain through small gasps of air, I look up and see Gena with two tears slowly streaming down her face and her eyes glassy. In the past, I had people just sit with me silently while I cried or hold me, but never had I seen someone cry with me. She made it more real and showed me it was okay to feel that way, to cry as much as I needed. What a powerful thing,

I thought, for someone else to cry with you when the pain really only has to do with your own life and not theirs. Such compassion and empathy she showed to take some of my suffering upon herself. She felt for me so much that she cried. I simply cannot forget that gift she has given me.

It took me years to figure out that being able to fall apart, really allowing yourself to do it and asking for help is the largest form of strength you could give to yourself. Asking for someone to hold you and walk beside you takes courage and strength in order to be able to say I just cannot do this on my own anymore. When it gets that bad, where the pain is just unbearable and you don't think you'll make it or you don't want to make it, inject yourself with a heavy dose of courage, ask and let someone lighten the burden of life. I think you'll find, in time, that a jolt of true inner strength will follow. I only wish I wasn't as stubborn earlier on to have learned this great lesson. Gena taught me that!

Missing

"The more you praise and celebrate your life,
the more there is in life to celebrate."
~ Oprah Winfrey ~

After you lose a loved one there's always one thing, one subject of matter that takes a bit longer than the rest of the process of grieving. It could be that you left something unsaid, or you just can't return to a certain location because it hurts too badly. Whatever the case or situation may be, it's okay. Some things take much longer than others to work through, let it be. And it may not feel okay that you've felt miserable about certain things for so long, why would it? You just can't understand why this one thing keeps dragging you down at times. Why? This is the question we ask. Why does it linger so badly and what have I done wrong along the way to have made it stay?

Stop.

Close your eyes and take a deep breath. It's not easy to throw yourself into the middle of the pain, thoughts and questions that just won't seem to go away. It's overwhelming once you get thinking on it because you put yourself inside of a never-ending loop of questions. What's wrong with me? Why couldn't I have? What if I had? And, Why can't I just…?

Of all the things that I worked through after Chris died, what bothered me most, what I never seemed to get away from, was the fact that my birthday was only days after I found out I'd no longer have him in my life. How incredibly painful it was to know that I had made it to another year of life while my brother had lost his. It was torture every year to know that a day of life and a day of death nearly overlapped each other, and always would. This was my biggest obstacle and I felt overwhelmingly guilty for being alive, for having my birthday so close to his death. No matter how much I told myself that Chris could only die once, in that specific year, it haunted me when every February came around. It was as if he actually died every year on that very day and the pain I felt lingered over into my birthday.

With only two full days in between the day he died and my birthday, my mind couldn't transition fast enough from one extreme emotion to another, which would always mean I was left with whatever debris was left over from the agonizing pain caused by his death. My birthday had become a day I dreaded because I honestly didn't know if there would ever come a year where I would be able to celebrate like most everyone else celebrates his or her birthday. Some years I was truly bitter for the fact this happened to me, and other years I could feel the child in me wanting to celebrate and be happy, although I never let it. The guilt of feeling happy superseded the feeling itself. I wondered what would have happened if my birthday had come just days before his death and if I would have been able to celebrate in the years following because I felt joy and happiness that would linger over into the day of his death, rather than the other way around. I would never know.

For years I had people ask what was wrong with me. Why don't you just have fun? Some would ask and then say, "He would want you to be happy, you know." It bothered me when people told me that. I knew he would want me to be happy, but you just can't feel something because someone wants you to. Others truly and honestly tried to make the best of my birthday for me. One year, a surprise party was thrown for me, other years, some went out of their way to make me a special cake, and another year a very dear friend took me out for a beautiful dinner and an evening out watching the sunset. My friend, Kelly, would send pink roses to me every year on my birthday and bought a star in the sky for my brother.

How grateful I am to each and every one of them for the effort and desire that they wanted something more for me, but there was still something missing, I felt it. I had myself convinced that it was Chris, who I'd never be able to get back. Even Tim spent three years doing everything in his power to make my birthday even better than the year before, and boy did he know how to outdo himself. It wasn't until the fourth year I spent with Tim that I really learned what had been missing all those years…

Life's Most Precious Gift

"Where there is great love, there are always miracles."
~ Willa Cather ~

"Good morning, beautiful, happy birthday," was the first thing I woke up to with such a deep smile on my face. I was happy and I knew it. I had secretly been pretty excited for this day; my twenty-fourth birthday and I let it show at certain times throughout the day. I still hadn't mastered not feeling guilt for being happy and so those moments came and left fairly quickly.

Tim had planned an early evening spending time with him and Gena's family. He knew I just loved spending time with their two little kids and I appreciated that he factored them into my day. How precious they were to me and I thoroughly enjoyed being able to blow out my candles, with a four-year-old, on the cake that Gena had made me. Seeing a child get so excited over birthday candles kept me in tune with my own inner child; I couldn't help but radiate out happiness in those moments. After we had cake, I opened my gifts that Gena gave me and, quickly after, Tim was whisking me away to the next part of my night.

We met up with some of my friends for the evening, one of which shared the same birthday month. Because my birthday was at the very beginning of March, this would start the countdown to his birthday. How outwardly he showed his excitement and wasn't afraid of what others thought of that. His joy intrigued me and, to be honest, was quite infectious. For the last few hours of my twenty-fourth birthday I found myself overjoyed to be living and at the same time regretful that I hadn't allowed myself to feel this way in years prior or that it had been too late to feel that excitement, the anticipation of this particular birthday; it was practically over.

At the end of the night, Tim and I went back home and I plopped myself down on the bed with a sigh; one you might hear at the end of a long but good day. "Don't you want your present from me?" Tim asked with enthusiasm. He was always excited to give me gifts and I loved the way he watched me, like a little kid, waiting for my reaction. I sat straight up on the bed, "Yes!" I said gently, but with excitement as I reached for his hand to squeeze. He made me close my eyes and put my hands out. I felt a cute little square box drop into my cupped hands with two cards. Sometimes Tim and I couldn't decide whether to get the mushy or funny card, so we got both! I opened my eyes and there it was, a white box with a bow that encased a black velvety box. Inside, it held a pair of earrings that I will always treasure, for the very fact that they remind me of this particular birthday. They were white gold, open heart-shaped diamonds; "They are absolutely beautiful, Tim." He smiled as he sat next to me, "Not as beautiful as you."

I couldn't help but try them on immediately and while I put them on in the mirror, I made mention to Tim about how excited my friend seemed to be about his birthday coming up. "Yeah," Tim said. "Because he wants to be." I turned around, showing off my earrings as if he hadn't seen them before, when I quickly realized that Chris hadn't really been a part of my day. There was no sulking or self-pity, and I hadn't felt that incredible longing for him until right at that very moment.

Tim saw the sudden change in my facial expression and knew exactly what was going on, as he began to speak. "I know you miss him. I'm sorry." He paused and walked over to where I was now sitting in his desk chair. He leaned down behind me and wrapped his arms around my shoulders. "You know," he began softly, "I can get you so many great things and make your birthday as fun as possible but I'm not sure it'll make you happy." I knew where he was going with it and just kept listening. "I know you appreciate all that people do but no matter what anyone does you're never going to enjoy today unless you truly *want* to and then *allow* yourself to; you're torturing yourself." I opened my mouth to speak but he continued in the same soft voice he had been using. "I mean, don't get me wrong, I think you've come a really long way even since the years I've known you. You used to not even *want* to be happy, but I see it now on your face and at times you push it aside like you shouldn't feel that way. It's okay to feel happy on your own birthday. It's okay." He squeezed me and then made me say it with him; "It's okay to feel happy on my own birthday." Two tears fell from my face.

He was absolutely right, every word. I was torturing myself. Tim made me realize what I had been missing for far too long; the joy of living itself. I had honestly forgotten what it had felt like to be happy for myself that I'm alive, that my life made even the smallest of difference in the world. It took me just under ten years after Chris died to be able to truly celebrate myself and allow the excitement to show. I felt free from the chains I, in fact, had put myself in but hadn't known it.

I owe my freedom from those chains, the celebration of my own life, primarily to Tim and the love he gave me regarding my life. He taught me that I don't *need* anyone to make my birthday better, not even him. As long as I am capable of allowing myself to truly celebrate, those around me are automatically going to double the joy I already have. I don't think I've ever received such an amazing gift. And to think, it was wrapped within myself; someone just had to tear an opening for me to see it was there.

"I love you with all my heart, Michelle." Somehow, fully loving somebody and the words "I love you" had so much more meaning, and always will for me, after knowing what it truly means to celebrate and love yourself.

Wounded Healer

"We can't control our destiny, but we can control who we become."
~ Anne Frank ~

I learned more about myself in my two years of grad school than I did in high school and undergrad combined. The words certain professors and supervisors chose to use really struck home, at times making me think for days about the meaning of the statement in my own life. I always thought grad school would be hard work and digesting a lot of information but I never thought I'd spend half my time analyzing my own life.

One professor taught me that as counselors we are the stagehand and our client is the director as well as actor; pain is a teacher that we need to allow the director to experience for him or herself. While we want nothing more than for someone to take the pain away for us, to direct us, it only starts to fade when we take on that burden of pain ourselves. One thing I've learned in life because of my own pain is to always be kind. There isn't one person out there who isn't fighting through his or her own just as painful burden. I may not be able to control what happens to others or myself but I sure can control who I become because of it and how I affect somebody else's day. It's easy to get caught up in your own pain to the point where you forget that others feel, too. You are not alone in feeling pain.

The other who taught me just as much about counseling, about life, was my supervisor at an internship site. He was incredibly intelligent and very wise. I enjoyed listening to every word he said. I'm sure you have or had someone in your life be so profound that they change a part of who you are, for the better. Without even knowing my story, or anything about my past, he was sharing some of the best advice anyone could give me if they had actually had known about my past and what had happened to me.

He first shared with me what it means to be in the counseling profession and how each counselor has their own story about why they chose to enter such a mentally challenging field, but what struck me was the way he chose to describe such people, including himself and me. "We are all wounded healers," he described, "who, at times, throw ourselves out there to heal others, knowing that their wounds were once our own at some point in our lives. We are setting the path for new healers, just as the healers before our time did for us."

I learned from him that as human beings we cannot omit pain, battle wounds or scars but we are never defeated if we can still play that one music note, dance that one move, write that one word, still use that one splash of color or complete that one sports play that make us who we are. Maybe you haven't quite finished the game, or composed an entire song…yet, but you still exist. And this is why you should always take time to celebrate yourself, truly in the core, because the wounds will consume you otherwise.

Time's Truth

"A human life is a story told by God."
~ Hans Christian Anderson ~

Time moves torturously slow…

As I was graduating from grad school, my sister Anna was just graduating from high school and Matt was finishing up his freshman year of high school. It made me happy that the two of them were close enough in age that they got to experience a year in school together. That was something I had always wanted and looked forward to with Chris but was unable to have, and the years there in high school felt like decades without him. That gap between Anna and I, that hole that Chris left us with, still seemed so large and didn't begin to close itself up until Anna went away to college, nine years after Chris died.

Nine years. Had it really been that long? Seemed only yesterday I sat in that hospital room, waiting to hear that the doctors couldn't save my brother's life. Time is everything yet means absolutely nothing at the same time. Did my pain dissipate over time? Sure, that's where time means everything, as much as I may not want to admit it. But even if I had eternal life, time will never bring back my brother, ever. For that, I hate time, and it means nothing when you can't get someone back. I hate time because for as long as I am alive, each hour, day, month, year that goes by is that much more time that I have to face knowing my brother could have been here. He's gone…time doesn't change that.

Although time could never bring Chris back, and at certain moments in my life I felt like time had frozen or paused just to torture me, I knew time was inevitably continuing on that regular, steady beat it always has despite my feeling of it speeding up or slowing down. Time would continue to change the seasons year after year. It would change people's faces and their age, and the more time that would pass, the memories of my brother for every single person that knew him would fade.

I thought about all the people in this world that would never get a chance to meet him and how the family members that were born after he died would only hear stories and distant memories of who Chris was and still is to our hearts. It saddens me that most of my cousins were too young or not yet born to remember my brother. Oh, how he loved to play with all of them and joke around. He loved to play manhunt with his cousins and tease them about monsters in the basement. For many of our cousins, he was a big brother none of them would have. Family was very important to Chris and if there's one thing I could leave with my cousins, it would be to always remember that, for Chris, we came first…family always came first.

The stories that have been shared in these pages and the many others that family and friends will continue to share, these are what I hope Christopher will be remembered and known for by those who never got the chance to really know him. No matter how much time surpasses you, never stop telling your most favorite memories of your loved one; they are treasures kept in the cave of your mind, share the wealth.

Time passes too quickly.

The Hope of Tomorrow

"I still miss those I loved who are no longer with me but I find I am grateful for having loved them. The gratitude has finally conquered the loss."
~ Rita Mae Brown ~

Why is it that people tell us after a death we need closure? Or when we explain to others that it just plain and simply hurts, they say things like, "Oh, you haven't gotten that closure yet, huh?" When these types of statements were said to me, regardless of when, I felt very abnormal, as if I wasn't doing the "right" things to heal. I think people expect those who grieve to cry it out, releasing it from the body and then it's as if you've closed the portal of pain pouring out of you and there is none left. It's "all better" and you can continue on.

I'm not so sure we ever close a door to those we've lost. If we did, it would be as though they never existed. Even those who try their hardest to shove the door closed, denying they ever had such a person in their life can never fully close that door. Once someone enters your life, regardless of how or when, good or bad, they have forever made their own imprint in the vault of your memory and ultimately contributed to who you are over time. There's no taking that away.

Closure means the end, something that was given finality. For those who have lost a sibling and for those who have lost any loved one, you know that the loss they left you with never really ends, does it? They are always going to be gone but that doesn't mean the pain doesn't fade. The excruciating hurt, the feeling that your chest is going to collapse turns to an ache. The ocean of tears that you cry becomes a puddle of leftover raindrops. Your broken heart learns to fuse itself back together but it's still bruised and there will forever be some form of scar left where your heart was torn. The loss becomes more livable.

Enduring a loss is much like a flowing river. For the most part, over time, it flows fairly calm and steady, and then there are days where the river runs low and there's not much there to speak of. But even today, ten years after Chris died there have been a few days where my river overflows and it rushes at me with rapids. I will always miss my brother, that's without question. But I've learned how to swim with the current when the waters are high. I laugh, I smile, I cry and I'm thankful for being given the opportunity of having my brother, Christopher, in my life for twelve years. What a strange but soothing feeling it is to sit here today and have more gratitude than pain, more laughs than tears. I am in love with life! One day, your tomorrows will become my todays, and when you get there, smile! That's when it's time for you to now pass on what you've learned to someone in your life that needs you just as badly as you needed someone to come into yours. You are among the wounded healers.

Today it hurts tremendously and you may feel like it'll never get better, even in the slightest. Tomorrow is a new day. Time drags on and the day seems endless. Eventually, tomorrow has to come. But today, you finished this book; we made it through together, to these very last words. Tomorrow you'll open a new book, a new chapter and maybe sometime in your tomorrows you'll come back and revisit these previous chapters that got you through life, and also some chapters you still need to work through. That's okay…one day at a time. Tomorrow may still hurt, but it's a new day.

Tomorrow is a new day.

Epilogue

I opened my eyes one morning, snuggled in a nice warm bed and quickly remembered I was back home, at my parents' house, visiting. When I got up and walked to the main floor of their house, the sun was shining brightly into all the windows just like on any beautiful spring day. Nobody had been up yet, not even the dog curled up in the living room rocking chair. I surveyed the house, looking out the windows in each main room. Something caught my attention as I passed by the dining room and so I went to that window that overlooks the backyard.

It amazed me how much sunlight was shining in our backyard in the morning, as the sun rises towards the front of our house. I stood there just admiring the way the yard looked. Sometimes, if you timed it right, you could see a family of deer eating towards the back of the yard. As I'm waiting to see if the deer will come, I take notice to Chris' weeping willow tree, as the sun shifted and hit it so eloquently. I lost myself through that windowpane, just staring at how beautiful this tree had become to me in those moments. The tree had just started budding its green leaves and pretty white flowers. It made me smile, knowing that new things were to come. It was at this moment, the title for the book I had been writing came to me, *Weeping Willow*. The tree remains the same, as beautiful as ever, planted firmly in the ground where it belongs, in the backyard of my childhood where I grew up with *three* siblings.

"How lucky I am to have known someone who was so hard to say goodbye to."
~ Unknown ~

Writing *Weeping Willow* was one of the most fascinating, inspiring, and fulfilling journeys I've ever been on. I learned so much about myself and about what parts of my grieving I really still needed to work on. Some of these chapters, especially the ones that forced me to recall minor details, were challenging to write, so much so that I had to get up from writing, walk away and process what I had just taken out of my head and put into words. For the most part, I remember these memories linearly but there are certain stories I don't quite remember when they occurred in the time line, possibly, because of all the trauma. It's difficult and at times heartbreaking to relive the pain and those moments that send shivers through your spine. I wouldn't change any of what I went through while *Weeping Willow* was being written. I am who I am because of it. Certain names were changed in the book to give those who wanted it their privacy.

My brother Matthew is now seventeen, Anna is twenty and I am twenty-six. Christopher would have been twenty-four. My parents are still happily married over thirty years and continue to endure their loss together. A lot has changed just within the past year and a half after completing *Weeping Willow*. My own health declined for quite some time until I was able to get the treatment necessary; a completely separate journey I had to bear. After just under five years of dating, Tim and I are no longer together. I firmly believe he entered my life to remind me of that love and joy I once had for life itself. There are others in this story that have come and gone in my life for whatever reasons, but they all had an impact on my life for which I'm grateful. Although they are no longer in my life and doors have closed, I am filled with joy for the amount of new and exciting doors that have already opened. I embrace each moment and am grateful for those who have recently entered my everyday life. You bring nothing but happiness.

Never did I think I'd be here today, ten years after Chris died, with a finished book and down a completely different path than what I originally intended or even along the way. After getting my Master's I became a NYS EMT, something I should have done years ago, but I am glad I'm doing it now. It's never too late to do something you've always wanted to do. It pairs so perfectly with my degree in counseling. I love what I do and I'm very happy with where this journey of mine has taken me. It surely has been one interesting roller coaster ride. Life is only what you make it to be.

Acknowledgments

First and foremost, I thank God for this opportunity to share with the world my story. I cannot thank the people who have helped make this book possible enough! I have always wanted to write a book on my experience but never had the courage to do so. Thanks to the loving support of family, friends, and colleagues, this book is here today.

I thank Dr. Peter Ladd for helping me with the process of writing a book and the push to do so, having faith in my abilities; it is mainly because of him that I even started writing. To Len Cornacchia, for the major help he gave in regards to publishing questions. *Weeping Willow* would not be the same and not nearly as good without the help and input of close friends such as Lauren Gumpel, Roman Shurp, Roberta and Tasha Velichko, Shawn Sigler, and Evan Sokal. The hours you all spent listening to me ramble are appreciated full-heartedly and can never be forgotten; you are the definition of true friends.

To my cousin, John Kalish, for the support and the precious time he took out of his life to make sure the book was how I intended it to be. I don't think you'll ever know how special you are to me. Thanks to those who edited, the world needs more people like you, with such patience. I'd probably still be working on this book if it weren't for those who spent time searching quotes with and for me. To all of you who have contributed, you've made this book complete, including all those who put a lot of hard work into the book from Author House.

Although a majority of the people already thanked are from the class of 2003, I'd like to thank the class as a whole for the support and little things so many of you did and continue to do without knowing the positive impact you had on my life. What an incredible class we have. You all remain in a very special place of my heart. In particular, to Vito Dimatteo Jr. for the support, happy memories, and love you've brought to my life.

Thank you to those who unconditionally showed their support and love, and never let me down when it came to my grieving process. Here's to Frank Oudheusden for all the memories we made with Chris and for being an extended brother. Anna and Matt, thank you for continuing to make me laugh. I look forward to future memories and stories that make us double over with laughter. I thank God for you both every day.

To all those mentioned in the book, I thank you for being a part of my life, this journey of mine, and for contributing to who I am today. I am forever in debt to all of you for the impact you've had on my life.

With all my love and gratitude,
Michelle

Weepingwillowloss@hotmail.com

Write with questions, comments, or if you'd like to connect with another who has lost a sibling.

www.ingramcontent.com/pod-product-compliance
Ingram Content Group UK Ltd.
Pitfield, Milton Keynes, MK11 3LW, UK
UKHW040602210726
13854UKWH00008B/1838

9 781463 438982